HE SPEAKS OUR LANGUAGE

The Story of an Irish Missionary in the Australian Outback

by Rob Douglas

• • • • • • • • • • • • • • • • • • •

Based on the Memoirs and featuring the sketches of
Wilfrid Henry Douglas

Aboriginal and Torres Strait Islander readers are advised that this book contains the names and details of people who have died. The names have been included with great respect for the way they influenced Wilf Douglas and the great contribution they made to the history of their own people.

Ark House Press
PO Box 1321, Mona Vale NSW 1660
Australia
Telephone: +61 2 9007 5376
PO Box 47212, Ponsonby, Auckland
New Zealand
Telephone: +64 9 416 8400
arkhousepress.com

© Rob Douglas

All rights reserved. No part of this publication may be reproduced, stored in a retrieval system or transmitted in any form or by any means electronic, mechanical, photocopying, recording or otherwise without the prior written permission of the publisher.

Cataloguing in Publication Data:
Title: He Speaks Our Language
ISBN: 978-0-9925192-7-8 (pbk.)
Subjects: Biography
Other Authors/Contributors: Douglas, Rob

Design and layout by initiatemedia.net

Wilfrid Henry Douglas Self-Portrait c.1944

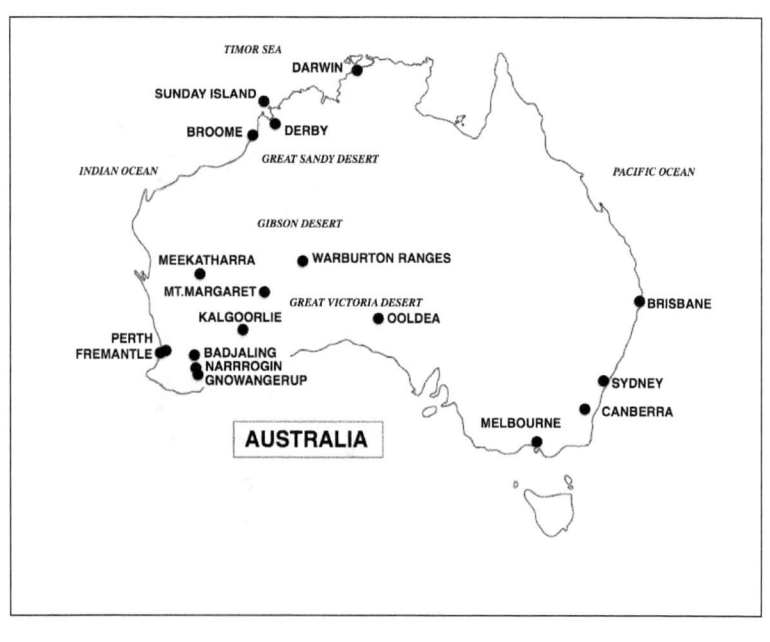

TABLE OF CONTENTS

1. Wheatbelt Pilgrimage — 1
2. Whirlpool Nightmare — 5
3. There's a Kid Missing — 17
4. Son of an Orangeman — 23
5. The Colonel's Eyes — 33
6. Lessons in Nyungar — 45
7. The Lone Scout — 55
8. Down the Line to Badjaling — 67
9. Joining the Military — 75
10. Natives in Church — 81
11. Kimberley Bound — 93
12. Sunday Island — 99
13. Journey to the Desert — 111
14. Writing the Stories — 121
15. Towards Independence — 129
16. Cycling the Goldfields — 139
17. Desert Moon — 149
18. Wilfrid Henry Douglas Bibliography — 155
19. Afterword — 161

1
Wheatbelt Pilgrimage

I called it a pilgrimage. It was the journey I had to have — a "back to your roots" sort of trip. For me there were no romantic flights to far distant lands, but a drive with my two adult sons, to an isolated Aboriginal community in the Western Australian wheatbelt. As we drove past the sign that announced we were entering the Badjaling Nyungar Community, I knew that I was stepping back into a history that was not only of significance to my family, but of deep significance to the Nyungar people.

Badjaling is situated about 200km east of Perth and about 12km beyond the tiny wheatbelt community of Quairading. It was originally a railway siding, a basic concrete platform that served as a staging place for wheat farmers to load their grain on to carriages to be railed to the port of Fremantle. Now there is no sign of the railway siding and the silent train tracks are overgrown. The mission that had once been established next to the railway siding was closed in 1954 and any buildings, including the wheat silos, were removed.

In recent years, a few families have returned to Badjaling and some houses have been built to restore a sense of community. My sons and I had come to Badjaling to meet some of the Nyungar elders and their families and to piece together some of my family history. Earlier in Quairading, we met a local Nyungar elder, Myrtle Yarran, and her son Norman. Myrtle and Norman invited us to follow them, so my sons and I got into our own car and headed off on the lonely road following Myrtle and Norman as they drove their own vehicle to Badjaling. Myrtle was a key link in the story that was about to be told.

As Myrtle, Norman, other elders, interested family members, and friends welcomed us to Badjaling, they were keen to take us for a walk through the bush to a clearing where a large piece of granite took pride of place. The stone, with a plaque attached, marked the location of what had once been a church that doubled during the week as a school. My father, Wilf Douglas, who had once taught children who were now elders in their community, had unveiled this plaque in November 1986 to honour nearly forty Nyungar families who had attended the school between 1930 and 1954.

Following the proclamation of the Swan River Colony in 1829, the Nyungar people—the original inhabitants of the southwest corner of Western Australia—discovered they were no longer seen as the proud protectors of the land they had loved for many generations. The people who had come onto their land had brought opportunities with them, but there were limits to who could benefit from these opportunities.

Government policy had sought to "breed out the black" and children were taken from their parents in an effort to prevent intermarriage between full blood Aboriginal people and those who were of mixed parentage. Parents lived in fear of the welfare officers who would arrive unannounced to pluck children from them and take them away to government or church-owned settlements, where many would be lost to their families forever.

The Nyungar people in the Western Australian wheatbelt were not allowed to attend the government school or hospital in Quairading. Such opportunities that were available to the farmers and more recent pioneers of this land were not available to the original inhabitants. Disappointed that children could not benefit from the local school and in fear of losing these children to the welfare system, two Irish missionaries who were living in the area were asked to consider starting a school.

Mary Belshaw and May McRidge began their school in the middle of a paddock at Dedaring. They chose this highly visible location because they wanted people to see that they had nothing to hide, and that they could be trusted not to betray anyone to the government at a time when the visit of welfare workers meant children would be taken away from their parents. Later they moved their school to the nearby railway siding at Badjaling where a school was established in a bough shed.

Shortly after moving into Badjaling, the bough shed was replaced by a building that was to double as a church and a school, built by the men of the community from flattened kerosene tins and wheat sacks sewn together. Three years later the wheat silo burst and the corrugated iron the silo had been constructed with became available at sixpence a sheet so the men took the opportunity to replace their old church and school with a more substantial building made out of corrugated iron.

In 1930, soon after their move into Badjaling, Miss Belshaw and Miss McRidge, as all knew them, received some unexpected help. Elizabeth (Beth) Weir was an eighteen-year-old girl from Perth who came to work for them as a housemaid. A sickly girl—Elizabeth's parents thought the country air would be good for her—so arranged for her to assist the spinster missionaries in their Christian ministry for the next two years.

As Myrtle Yarran pointed to where the old church used to stand, my mind wandered to the experiences of that eighteen-year-old girl who was to become my mother some twenty-two years later. Amidst the heat and flies and the sparse scrub that was so different from her home in the Perth suburb of Bayswater near the banks of the Swan River,

He Speaks Our Language

Miss Weir was to develop a love for the Nyungar people of Badjaling. Her love for these people was to follow her for more than fifty years of service to Aboriginal people around Australia. After two years she was to leave Badjaling to study at Perth Bible Institute.

Wilfrid (Wilf) Douglas was one of the young men at the institute when Beth arrived. A few years younger than Beth, Wilf dreamed of becoming a missionary to China. That dream would never be fulfilled, but after two years at the college, Wilf would find himself at the isolated railway siding of Badjaling and the beginning of a journey that would see him playing a pivotal role in the preservation of Aboriginal languages across Australia. Having been whisked away from his family in Northern Ireland as a child and facing a new life thousands of kilometres from family and friends, Wilf was destined to meet Beth again some years later and spend their lives together working selflessly for the benefit of people, many of whom were to become known as the "Stolen Generation".

Rob Douglas

FOOTNOTE: The spelling Nyungar was originally used by Wilf Douglas and is in common use in Perth. The spelling Noongar was supported by Great Southern people at a meeting in Narrogin in 1992 and remains in common use on the South coast and Great Southern regions of W.A.

2
Whirlpool Nightmare

A slightly battered wooden pearling lugger was anchored in glistening, azure waters a short distance from the red dirt and harsh outcrops of a craggy island that reached out of the water towards the fiery sub-tropical sun. The sweat dripped from the forehead of Alec, a sinewy Bardi man as he rolled up the ropes and made sure the dinghy was securely lashed to the back of the lugger in preparation for a trip across the treacherous waters of the Dampier Peninsula in the far north of Western Australia. Alec, an elder in the community, had grown up on Iwanya, the largest of a group of islands known as the Sunday Islands, but like most people, just referred to Iwanya as Sunday Island.

Alec had a competent crew of men and Bardi speaking people from Sunday Island, who were familiar with the journey through Sunday Strait, a narrow entrance passage to King Sound, which led 120km south to the isolated township of Derby nestled at the base of the sound. They were used to fishing and hunting for trochus shell throughout the Buccaneer Archipelago, manoeuvring vessels through brittle coral and dangerous rocks.

Wilf Douglas had arrived at Derby in 1947 with his wife, Beth, and newborn son, John, to work with the United Aborigines Mission, and after a short time had moved to Sunday Island, a tiny outcrop about five kilometres long and two kilometres wide. It was the home to about 200 Aboriginal people. In a short time, they were the only non-Aboriginal people living on the island and discovered there were some spoken and unspoken expectations about what it meant to be the sole missionary family. Handling the business of purchasing supplies from Derby was one of those responsibilities, though getting to Derby on the mission lugger, the *Balfour Matthews,* depended on the expertise of men who had generations of experience traversing these waters in mangrove tree catamarans, and knew practically every reef, rock, shoal and current in the surrounding seas.

The Bardi people had told Wilf about four-masted schooners that had disappeared in the whirlpools of Sunday Strait, so there was a level of nervousness for Wilf as he watched Alec and the other men preparing the lugger for sailing. The *Balfour* had been battered by a recent cyclone, but a trip to Derby had become critical as food supplies in the mission store were dwindling. The people had become addicted to the government rations of flour, tea and sugar—especially to sugar. The sugar supply ran out first, and the situation became tense when news came through from Derby that the state ship which was to bring new supplies from the south of the state had been delayed in Fremantle.

After several days, news came by pedal radio that the state ship *Dorrigo* had been able to get away from Fremantle and was on its way to Broome. When the men heard the news, they rounded up a crew and urged Wilf to take the lugger to Derby to collect the stores as soon as the ship arrived there. The men were ready to risk the trip despite the poor condition of the lugger, and while he was not keen to leave his wife and young son alone on the island, Wilf agreed to make the trip.

At noon the *Balfour*, towing a small dinghy, chugged away from the deep water anchorage at Sunday Island. Its ancient four-stroke marine engine seemed almost too powerful for the weakened timbers below the waterline. Wilf's task was to keep the little engine going. The navigation was the responsibility of the Bardi men who knew these waters better than he knew the streets of Perth.

As Wilf watched Alec managing the sails on the lugger he recalled an earlier incident in his relationship with Alec. The Sunday Island people considered it a shame to get angry too quickly, so any disagreements between families would be discussed at length, often for up to two weeks. Then, when everybody understood the issues clearly and a resolution had not been reached, a boomerang would be thrown at one of the huts. This was a signal for the whole camp to grasp spears and boomerangs and join in the fight. These conflicts were sometimes like an all-out war with boomerangs and spears flying and hand-to-hand fighting with hitting sticks, crowbars or pieces of timber.

Beth and Wilf had become aware a fight was looming. They were awaiting the arrival of the lugger with new medical supplies and became concerned that the fight would break out before the supply of bandages arrived. Boomerang and spear wounds can be quite serious, so Wilf walked into the middle of the northern camp, stood on a high rock, and called the people to attention. He told the crowd before him that he was aware that a fight was almost due to start, but appealed to everyone to hold off until the lugger arrived with more medical supplies. He even threatened not to treat anybody if they got wounded before the boat arrived.

While he was talking, someone threw a boomerang at a hut. Within seconds, over a hundred people filled the campsite while women and children ran up the hill to escape the flying boomerangs and spears. Wilf was caught in the middle of the conflict, but decided to run in amongst the fighters and try to stop two men who were facing each other belligerently with spears. He managed to separate them and while they shook hands with each other, the battle was still going on around them. Boomerangs flew over their heads and voices were yelling from the hillside, "Mr. Douglas, Mr. Douglas, come away ... quick...you'll get killed."

At dark, the noise of the conflict settled down so Beth and Wilf went to bed, but at midnight a loud knocking awakened them. "Come quick, Mr. Douglas, the blood's running out of Old Alec's head," the late night visitors called out. Wilf reminded them of his threat not to treat anybody wounded because they were short of bandages, but when he realised the nature of the wound, he gave the relatives a gauze pad and some antiseptic and told them to keep the pad pressed on the wound.

About one a.m. there was another call. "Mr. Douglas, the blood's still running out of Alec's head." This time, he got a hurricane lantern and followed the people to Alec's hut. He was sitting in the low doorway clothed in a blood-congealed military overcoat. It would have been difficult to shave the hair away in the poor light, but the wound had stopped bleeding. It was high on his forehead, so Wilf put another gauze pad on it and got him to lie down on his mattress with his head raised. He turned to Alec's son: "If it bleeds again, put pressure on the wound and in the morning we'll shave away the hair and dress the wound properly."

The wound on Alec's head cleared up nicely, so Wilf was surprised some weeks later when a deputation arrived at their door announcing that Alec was dying. Wilf went with them immediately to Alec's camp and found the old man lying on a blanket under a bough shade. After examining him and finding no sign of illness, Wilf asked his relatives why they thought he was dying. Finally, one of the women whispered that the men had pointed the bone at him.

Wilf had learned a little about the power of Aboriginal sorcery, but at this stage the only authority he had observed on the island was his own in what had become known as "the power of the flour". As acting superintendent of the Sunday Island Mission he was in charge of the store and this gave him an authority recognised by the men as one of great importance. He felt out of his depth in this situation, but breathed a prayer, pulled his shoulders back and walked over to what was commonly referred to as man's country to talk to the men who were gathered there. "Why did you point the bone at Alec?" he asked the men. It was a straightforward question, but he recognized he was dealing with tribal leaders and needed to show respect. A laugh circled the group of men and then a spokesman stepped forward and told him that nobody had seriously pointed the bone. "It was only a joke," someone explained.

Wilf was angry. It was obvious Alec had given up his will to live and was refusing to eat. "Alec doesn't see it as a joke," he retorted. "You need to come with me and speak to Alec." The whole group of men followed him over to the bough shade where Alec lay. They gathered around and eventually convinced him that he had nothing to fear. Within a few days he was his old self again.

Through this incident, Wilf and Alec had developed a mutual regard for each other that was to maintain them through the adventure they were soon to experience together.

A massive amount of water poured through the Sunday Strait, and ships could only approach the eleven metre high Derby jetty when it was high tide. At low tide any boats left standing at the jetty would be stranded on the mud unable to go anywhere until the next change of tide. The skills of people like Alec were necessary in traversing the strait and heading into the sound on the strong in-going tide. They passed Cunningham Point, about one-third of the distance to Derby, then the tide turned against them and the waters began pouring out of King Sound. With a slight breeze in the sails and the engine on full throttle, they barely held their position for the next six hours until the tide turned again at about midnight. A strong north wind filled their sails and, with engine going and the tide hurtling them along, they reached Derby jetty about eleven o'clock next morning, only to discover, to their surprise, that the *Dorrigo* was not there.

The township of Derby was a few kilometres walk from the jetty along a powdery marsh track, so Wilf, Alec and the rest of the crew made their way into town where they learned that the *Dorrigo* had missed the high tide at Broome and was stuck at the Broome jetty for about four days. They could see no value in heading back to Sunday Island with only emergency supplies, then returning in four days for the main store supply, so made inquiries about other ways they could transport necessary supplies to the island.

Australian Iron and Steel was mining at Cockatoo Island, another small island within the archipelago, and the men were told that the company's diesel-driven ship, the *Yampi Lass* was due to arrive at Derby jetty at three o'clock that afternoon.

As the bronzed skipper of the *Yampi Lass* climbed up the ladder from the workboat on to the jetty, a short, skinny white man with balding head, and an older Aboriginal man confronted him. The two strangers stepped forward as the mountain of a man pulled himself on to the jetty and towered over them. Wilf introduced himself and asked if there was any chance the *Yampi Lass* could take them back to Sunday Island to deliver some stores. The skipper listened quietly for a minute, then exploded, "Nothing will make me take my ship to Sunday Island. Don't you realise that one of those whirlpools in the strait could suck my ship under with my whole crew as well!"

In a tirade of colourful language, the skipper told Wilf and Alec how dangerous it would be for him to take his ship anywhere near Sunday Island, but as he and his men started to walk into Derby, he called back over his shoulder that if they weren't at the jetty at three o'clock the next morning they would be left behind. By 2:30 next morning, Alec and Wilf were waiting at the jetty with a seventy-pound bag of sugar, a bag of potatoes, and a few other necessities ready to greet about thirty drunk miners who were off to work at the iron ore mine on Cockatoo Island. They helped the men and the skipper, who was also intoxicated, into the workboat, then up the rope ladder to the deck of the *Yampi Lass*.

The sun was high in the sky when Wilf awoke and became conscious that the ship's engines had changed speed. All around was the roar of rushing water. Alec was already loading the stores on to the dinghy when Wilf reached the deck. A quick glance at the nearby island told him that they were not near Sunday Island, but were in the Fantome Pass, east of Mermaid Island. About seventeen kilometres separated Mermaid from Sunday Island with the treacherous waters of Sunday Strait in between. The captain who would not risk his own ship was about to lower two men and a dinghy into imminent danger.

As the dinghy was lowered into the swirling waters, it looked frighteningly small. Alec and Wilf climbed down the rope ladder to the dinghy and pushed it away from the ship. When the lines were loosed, the outgoing current hurtled them towards the rocky coast of Mermaid Island. Paddling furiously, they managed to break through the current and reach shallow water. Alec jumped overboard on to the coral reef and towed the dinghy closer to the shore so that Wilf, being shorter in the legs than Alec, could get out on the reef and help him tow the dinghy around the island to the western side opposite Sunday Island.

It took nearly two hours to reach the other side where they tied the boat to a mangrove tree and waited for the tide to turn. Meanwhile they climbed to high ground and lit a fire, so that the smoke would alert residents of Sunday Island they were on their way back.

About one p.m. the waters of the strait became quiet and glassy, a sign that the tide had stopped running out. "Slack water now," announced Alec, "we start paddling!" In the fifteen minutes before the tide began to run into the sound again, they cleared the Mermaid Island reef and began rowing the dinghy towards Sunday Island. Wilf prayed for Beth who, he figured, would have been told about the smoke signals and that they had begun the dangerous crossing. Sunday Island was clearly visible and it seemed they could be there in a short time.

After an hour of pulling the oar, Wilf's muscles were aching, and he wondered how long he could keep paddling. With his back towards the front of the dinghy, he couldn't see that they were drifting further and further south of Sunday Island. Slowly he began to realise, what his experienced companion knew all along, that the incoming tide was hurtling them further and further into King Sound away from their destination. By sundown, they were opposite Cunningham Point and further from Sunday Island than when they left Mermaid Island.

At slack water, they managed to cross the central stream and started back towards Sunday Island on the outgoing tide. They still needed to row or take turns sculling the dinghy to keep them from drifting into the centre of the strait. After sundown, a strong southeasterly breeze sprang up and whipped up the waves. In the fading light of day, the white-capped waves contrasted with the ominous blackness of the rocks that seemed to be peppered indiscriminately around the boat.

Then the whitecaps began to come into the dinghy and before long, their feet were covered with swirling bilge water. Alec sculled the boat, while Wilf fished around in the water trying to find a bailer shell. By the time he found the shell, his suitcase was beginning to float. He worked furiously to toss the water back into the sea, meanwhile struggling to save himself from being thrown overboard.

When most of the water was emptied out, they began rowing in unison again. The men's limbs were aching and the muscles in their backs were running hot with the friction—in spite of the cold wind and the salt sea spray.

The sea roared and the wind whistled in their ears as they sped on the outgoing current. Sunday Island was now looming up as a shadowy heap of rocks in the north. Volumes of water forced frothing streams over coral beds between rocks. Wilf knew he had an expert navigator on the boat with him; but prayed that he would soon be delivered from this fury of sea and wind.

In the rage of the sea, the whole world began to spin around them. The white caps of the waves, the dark rocks, the stars in the sky, the silhouetted islands on the horizon, everything whirled around them in a great blur of speed. Wilf looked at Alec sitting at the other end of the dinghy. He was still rowing, but the world was passing by him at a tremendous speed. Suddenly the truth hit ... they were floating across a whirlpool. Wilf looked down and saw the black hole below them with white seas spinning them around the top of the hole. Above the thunderous roar of the waters, Wilf yelled out to Alec, "What do we do now, Alec?" Calmly he shouted back, "Keep paddling, Mr. Douglas!"

As Wilf threw new energy into rowing, the dinghy shot forwards, out of the whirlpool and on to the outgoing current. Before he had the chance to ask Alec how far they had to go, his oar was twisted out of his hand and thrown across his lap. Again the world started its wild careering and Wilf became conscious of the black vortex of another whirlpool below them.

They spun around at a terrifying speed. Looking at Alec rowing rhythmically at the other end of the dinghy, Wilf got the impression that the boat was sitting motionless on the top of the whirlpool, but the whole universe outside was spinning around them in a rushing, noisy blur. Time stood still until the hypnotic effect of the movement was shattered by Alec's voice, "When we get back, you'll have to lend me this boat, Mr. Douglas!" The wall of the whirlpool appeared over the side of the dinghy then with a mighty lurch, they were thrown out of the black hole into a rushing stream. The boat literally screamed over coral beds and past protruding rocks.

In the meantime, back on the island, Beth arranged for some of the people to take a lighted hurricane lantern to what was known as Cocky's Camp, a rocky landing at the southern end of the island. As Alec and Wilf rowed hard under the starlit sky, surrounded by swirling waters and white-capped waves, they spotted the lantern light at Cocky's Camp. Its glow momentarily revealed the white dress of a woman who seemed to be holding a lantern aloft. Wilf shrieked towards the landing, but the mighty chorus of sea noises drowned his voice. High rocks between them and the shore quickly blotted out the light, and they were torn relentlessly towards Meda Pass and the Indian Ocean.

"Keep paddling, Mr Douglas," cried Alec. "If we miss Umbina, we'll be lost." The point of Umbina reaches out into Sunday Strait and is named Salvation Point. It was their last hope of touching land before they would be hurtled in the outgoing current to the Indian Ocean and more deadly whirlpools of the archipelago. The speed at which they were skimming through the churning sea, the deafening roar of the reef, and the fragility of the dinghy, all combined to produce a frenzied determination to keep paddling, in spite of exhausted limbs. Then without warning, Alec jumped up and out of the dinghy into the frothing sea. Wilf was taken by surprise; but in a moment realised that Alec was on his feet and holding on to the rope at the front of the dinghy. The boat swung around and faced the opposite direction, Alec with water up to his waist, was towing the dinghy over a coral reef to the sandy shore. His quick move had rescued them from speeding past their hope. They had landed at Salvation Point.

It was midnight, and it was impossible for them to make their way across the deep mud channel that separated Umbina from the main island. They found a place out of the chilling wind. Surprisingly, the matches in Wilf's suitcase were still dry, so they lit a fire and cooked a few potatoes in the ashes as they waited for dawn. It was midday next day before the tide was out far enough for them to pick their way around the edge of the coral reef to reach the main island. From the height of Iwanya came the shouts of welcome from a scouting party.

Wilf's life wasn't short of adventure, even before before these great sea adventures, and they certainly weren't the end. It all started many years earlier on the violent streets of Belfast, Northern Ireland, then in a surprise twist this young Irish boy found himself separated from his family forever, living in a village for migrant children nestled in bushland in the southwest of Western Australia.

3
There's a Kid Missing

The sergeant's voice calling from the back door of the stone police station awakened the dark-skinned man who was dozing under the shade of a tree. He quickly jumped to his feet. "There's a kid missing," the sergeant called again. Albert knew what he had to do straight away. He pulled on his boots, and along with two officers, headed north from the small township of Pinjarra towards a nearby farm school called Fairbridge. It wasn't the first time the police had been called to Fairbridge to try and find a fair-skinned British boy who had run away and was wandering in unfamiliar bushland.

Albert was an Aboriginal police tracker, and his skills in following footprints and other telltale signs were valued by the local police force. He had grown up in the Pinjarra area and knew the countryside intimately. He was a Nyungar man and his people had lived in the Pinjarra area, on the Murray River, about 100km south of Perth—the capital city of Western Australia—for as long as time could recall. Less than one hundred years before, this country had been the scene of what had become known as the Battle of Pinjarra. In retaliation for the death of one of his servants, the governor of the Swan River Colony, Captain James Stirling and a detachment of twenty-five soldiers and police travelled down from the colony in search of those who had been responsible. On October 28, 1834, Stirling came across the Murray River camp of the Binjdareb Nyungars. There were probably about eighty people at the camp and there were reports that up to fifteen Nyungars were killed in the sudden attack. Only one in Stirling's party died.

Albert had probably heard stories of the battle from his father and grandfather as they sat around the campfire at night, but this was the last thing on his mind. A boy had run away from Fairbridge. He had to do all he could to find him before he died of cold or starvation in a hostile landscape very different from his home in the northern hemisphere. As he searched, he wondered about Fairbridge, a neat village surrounded by farmlands with its very English buildings and institutional ways, planted in the middle of the Australian countryside. Why would a boy run away from a place like that? Could it be that he was being mistreated?

Wilf Douglas was a twelve-yeear-old Irish boy who lived in Fairbridge. He knew why Leslie Bishop had run away and so did the other boys who had been shipped to this isolated outpost of the British Empire, thousands of kilometres from their homes in the northern hemisphere. When Wilf and his friends saw the police arrive at Fairbridge, they watched from a distance to see what would happen. Two uniformed policemen were bustled into the staff dining room for refreshments. A third man, a dark-skinned man wearing a khaki uniform and a broad hat, was with them. The boys had never seen an Aboriginal Australian before, but something seemed odd to them that this man was left outside when his colleagues were taken into the dining room.

The boys ran up to him and asked:
"Did you find Bishop?"
"Yes I found him," replied Albert.
"Did you bring him back?" the boys asked.
"No," he replied. "I figured he must have had a good reason for running away so I gave him some tucker and put him on a train."

From that moment Wilf was filled with a great admiration for the Australian Aborigines.

Like Bishop, he was desperately lonely and homesick and would cry himself to sleep at night thinking about his loved ones back home in Belfast. Bishop was found a few days later and that night it was impossible to sleep. As Wilf tossed and turned in bed, he thought about the beating his friend had received in front of all the boys in the main dining hall by the principal, Colonel Heath, a one-armed former Grenadier Guard. He recalled another farm manager who had knocked a boy to the ground and kicked him for being late for dinner. The story the boys whispered to each other was that he used to be a slave driver in India.

In the silence of his bedroom Wilf replayed the booming military voice of the colonel as he entered the dining room each day, calling the children and their housemothers to order so they could say grace in unison before eating. In that moment he concocted a plan. Before he left the Belfast docks, the last time he would ever see his mother, he was given a New Testament by his mother's cousin, Esmee, and tucked inside was the address of an uncle who was an inspector with the Fremantle tramways. He quickly found the address and wrote a letter to his Uncle Harry O'Neill, telling him how he was feeling and asking him to rescue him. The next day he secretly approached a visitor to Fairbridge and asked the visitor to post the letter for him.

But the plan backfired. Harry O'Neill had never heard that he had a nephew at Fairbridge, so he was puzzled when he received the letter, particularly as he had only ever heard good things about the farm school, so he wrote a letter to Colonel Heath and included a note of reassurance to the boy who claimed to be his nephew.

At dinnertime, the matron of each cottage would sit at the head of the table and the children from that cottage would take their places around the table. The head matron, who was also the matron at Shakespeare girls' cottage, was nicknamed the black beetle because she always dressed in a long black dress with crocheted white-lace collar and cuffs. Her white hair was tied into a bun at the back and her small eyes, her sharp nose and gold-rimmed spectacles helped to strengthen her reputation for austerity.

Swedes, turnips, cabbage and spinach with boiled mutton and potatoes were the main items on the midday menu, followed by boiled rice, sago, tapioca, and bread pudding or occasionally dried apricots boiled and served with a thin custard, or rhubarb and custard. For breakfast the usual fare was oaten porridge, bread and white mutton dripping and a small amount of jam. They were forbidden from having jam and dripping on the same piece of bread, and if seconds of bread and jam were requested, the child would be sent to the servery where the head matron would dip a knife into a dish of watery red jam, wipe it on a thick slice of white bread, and hand the result back on a tin plate.

The buzz of voices and the clink of cutlery came to a sudden stop at the sound of Colonel Heath's voice. The children sat silently, wondering what to expect next.
"Douglas, come to the front."
Shaking with fear young Wilf moved to the front of the dining hall where a stranger accompanied the Colonel. The children sat silently, their spoons and forks suspended in mid-sentence as Colonel Heath called the whole assembly to order and introduced the chairman of the Perth Committee of the Child Immigration Society, Mr. Joyner. He then turned to the small Irish boy nervously standing next to him and said:

"Douglas! You wrote to some uncle in Fremantle asking to be taken away from Fairbridge?"
"Yes, sir."
"You were homesick at the time, were you not, Douglas?"
"Yes, sir."
"But you are not homesick now, are you Douglas?"

"No, sir."
"And you will never do this again, will you Douglas?"
"No, sir."
"Very well then, sit down!"

Still shaking in his shoes, Wilf made his way back to his seat. The children remained in silence as they finished their meal and filed out of the dining room, each one having heard the stern warning from the two most powerful men they knew that running away from Fairbridge was not an option.

Drew Memorial Parish Church and Elementary School, Belfast

4
Son of an Orangeman

The annual protestant "Orange" parade season had started in Belfast, Northern Ireland when Wilfrid Henry Douglas was born. It was the 4th of July 1917, and Sir Edward Carson had sent the men of his Ulster Volunteer Force to fight for Britain in Europe and Turkey. The bill granting Home Rule to Ireland had been passed in Westminster, but awaited the end of World War I to become effective. The following year, Sinn Fein would gain majority rule and form its own parliament, giving birth to the Irish Republican Army. Ireland was on the verge of six years of violent revolution.

Wilf's father Henry (Harry) Douglas was in France as a batman to Colonel Wilfrid Spender, acting GSO 1 of the 36th Ulster Division Royal Irish Rifles when Wilf was born. Harry had been saved from death by one of the Colonel's horses when a German sniper fired a shot at him, so decided to name his son after Wilfrid Spender.

Spender had previously signed the Ulster Covenant and was involved with Carson in the formation of the Ulster Volunteer Force (UVF). With Creighton Milne, of the Conservative Central Office, he started the Anti-Home Rule Petition. He was also involved in the gun-running activities intended to arm the UVF against the South or any British attempt to take over the government of Ulster.

He Speaks Our Language

As a youngster, Harry Douglas took Wilf to the "Clethers", Spender's stately home at Strandtown, where Sir Wilfrid took them for a walk around his property, and on the way, collected an egg from his poultry run. He asked Wilf how he spelt his name. When he answered with W-I-L-F-R-E-D, the colonel wrote WILFRID on the egg and handed it to his namesake with the instruction that this was how he was to always spell his name.

Wilf and his brother Woodrow, two years and three days his junior, lived in quarters at the back of Harry and Mina Douglas' hardware store in Burnaby Road, Belfast. When they fell on hard times the shop had to be sold and they moved to a house across the street. Harry belonged to the Loyal Orange Lodge and proudly taught his sons about what it meant to be a loyal Orangeman. He would put an orange sash around Wilf's neck and send him down to Sandy Row to watch the twelfth of July processions where the youngster was stirred by the pipe and drum bands, the beat of the big lambegs, the enormous drums with symbols of the Orange order painted on them, and the marching music played by the brass band and flutes. But there were some aspects of these events he didn't quite grasp. Such as why the men would break out of the procession and give him a shilling because he was a "brave boy" or why these loyal Orangemen would get drunk at "the fields" after the march.

Violence was commonplace on the streets of Belfast, and as he walked home that day in May 1929, a few months short of his twelfth birthday, he carefully avoided standing on a piece of paper or a cigarette packet on the footpath, as he had been taught, in case it was a concealed detonator. He walked past buildings that had been blown up and shops that had bullet holes in their windows. Street riots were familiar and the time that he was knocked down by a UVF armoured car during riots in the city was still fresh in his mind. On that occasion he was taken to hospital in the armoured vehicle with a fractured skull and broken shoulder blade.

As he walked home from school, Wilf thought about his mother. Mina Douglas was a somewhat shadowy figure in his early life. Somewhere in the past he had vague memories of a mother who would play classical music on the piano and violin, who would sketch and paint and even worked with her brother James in his architectural studio. But all that changed when Wilf was about three and Mina gave birth to her third child who died after three days. Mina was taken to hospital suffering from a stroke. She lost the use of her right hand and her speech was affected, then for reasons never explained to her eldest son, Mina was transferred to Purdeysburn Mental Hospital. Wilf didn't see her again for several years. He never really knew much about the hospital where his mother had gone, but it was common schoolyard banter to threaten to send someone to Purdeysburn if the children thought someone was a little different from what they considered to be normal.

On her return to the family home, as if to compensate for the years they had lost, Mina would take Wilf to visit places like the Opera House on Grosvenor Road and to a rustic bridge where she and Harry had courted each other and to places like Cave Hill, a natural prominence visible from almost any part of Belfast. On the way up the hill, they wandered through the Bellevue gardens, then walking up a steep path, they came to a stream of water gurgling its way down the hillside. With great difficulty Mina opened her handbag and took out a piece of writing paper and folded it into a cup shape. She bent down and scooped up some water and offered it to her son.

Wilf smiled as he thought about his mother, then the drab streets of Belfast brought him back to reality. In 1928, these memorable journeys that Wilf had with his mother were unexpectedly over. The economic depression hit, and Harry's customers couldn't pay their bills. Harry would keep Wilf home from school to collect his debts. He would knock on doors and would regularly hear from the women he visited, "I know who you are. You're Harry Douglas's boy. Tell your father my husband is still out of work and we've got no money."

Wilf used to collect postage stamps and trade them for conjuring tricks at a little shop on the other side of the city. His uncle Edmund was visiting when he came home with one of his new tricks. As he showed the family what he had earned through his trade, Uncle Edmund told him: "Instead of buying conjuring tricks, why don't you buy a loaf of bread for your mother?"

As he got closer to home, he began to think about the things people had been saying, the comments from his father's customers, and Uncle Edmond's cutting remark. He began to realise how critical their situation had become. Then, as he walked through the front door he saw Mina and Woodrow looking at photographs and brochures. Without warning Woodrow asked, "Would you like to go to Australia?" His brother and mother then began to show Wilf the brochures and photographs of cows in green paddocks and enormous fruit orchards. The pictures were a marked contrast to the dirty streets of Belfast, and his eyes widened as he flicked through the brochures, trying to grasp what they meant.

Still reeling from the unexpected information that seemed to be coming his way, Wilf was not yet ready for the news his father was to bring him when he came home that night from the Customs House where he was now working. Harry confirmed to his son that the Overseas League of Belfast had offered to send an Ulster boy to Australia. He had applied to the league, asking them to consider his eldest son, and was successful. If he was to go ahead and prepare the way, Harry assured his son, the rest of the family would join him the following year.

The story appeared in the *Belfast Telegraph* Saturday, May 25, 1929.

Overseas League Spirit

Ulster Boy for Australia (sic)

Wilfred Douglas, aged 11, was the guest of honour at an informal social meeting of the Overseas League on Friday afternoon.

Wilfred is the adopted son or "godchild" of the Ulster branch of the League, and his godparents are sending him to the Fairbridge Farm School, Western Australia, there to be trained to uphold the honour of the British flag and to help develop the resources of the Empire.

Wilfred sails for his new home on Monday.

Lady Katharine Hamilton, President of the League, wrote regretting her inability to be present, but she sent her godson a silver watch, which was presented to him by the Rt. Hon. H. M. Pollock.

Sir Frederick and Lady Cleaver, Lady Byers, Mrs. John M'Conigal, Miss M'Connell, Mr. Robert Baillie, Mrs. John M'Connell, Miss Corry, and the energetic Hon. Secretary, Miss Cowan, were amongst those who attended the little ceremony in the Club's headquarters at the Carlton.

As his father took him out the back door and down the back lane to the tram, Wilf didn't realise that he had said good-bye to his mother for the last time. Together, he and his father headed to the city to pick up a suitcase and some clothing, then down to the Belfast docks to board a ship that was to take them both to London.

Just as they were boarding, Wilf's cousin Esmee and her mother emerged from the crowds at the foot of the gangplank. Esmee was the daughter of Harry's cousin, John Douglas. She had been giving Wilf piano lessons and he had grown quite fond of her. She gave him a small New Testament in which she had written, "To Wilfrid, to remind you of your promise to write. Love, Esmee."

Those last minutes as the ship left the docks were a blur, but in the midst of the confusion, Wilf spotted his mother with her cousin, Auntie Annie Wishart, standing together waving their handkerchiefs.

Realising he was leaving mother and home, Wilf began waving wildly, but Harry quickly took him down to his cabin where he gave him some small gifts and got him ready for bed. At midnight, his father woke him, wrapped him in his greatcoat and took him up on deck to see the lights of Douglas, the capital city of the Isle of Man, then at six the next morning they pulled into the docks of Liverpool and hurried to catch the Express to London.

Harry accompanied Wilf to the Child Emigration Society Building and to Australia House. Children speaking many different dialects of English were crowded into the building, and it seemed there were far more children than adults. He tried to stay close to his father and through the noise he heard his father say, "Remember boy, always call a woman madam and a gentleman sir, and don't play cards." Someone was issuing instructions and adults were bringing plates of canned peaches around for the children to eat. In the confusion, Wilf realised that his father had disappeared. There was no farewell, and he was alone in the crowd.

His family was gone forever.

More confusion. More instructions. There was noise and children jostling for attention. Voices called them to order and before they knew what was happening, Wilf noticed he and the other children were being bundled into a train headed for Southampton. As he sat in the train everything seemed a blur as he tried to work out what had just occurred. Mighty steel structures passed by the windows of the carriage, along with cranes and dusty industrial buildings, then, without any warning about where they were going or what was happening to them, the train pulled into the Southampton Docks and outside the window was what appeared a great wall of blackness. The great hull of the *Larg's Bay* with black smoke pouring out of its funnel, was to transport thirty lonely British youngsters to a new world in Australia.

Leaving Belfast 1929

As he stepped out of the train and made his way up the gangplank of the *Larg's Bay*, Wilf looked up and saw the captivating smile of a woman welcoming each of the children aboard. Miss Marion Forbes was to be the matron-in-charge during their voyage to the other side of the world. Her cheery welcome and friendly smile gave him hope that someone had his interests at heart. Despite the last words of his father, Miss Forbes didn't want to be called madam, and she taught the boys to play cards. She was there as they sailed through the Bay of Biscay in calm seas and entered the Mediterranean, and as they passed the Rock of Gibraltar and the island of Malta. When a cloud of locusts descended on the boat, as they went through the Suez Canal, crew members mobilised the boys to collect the squirming locusts on the deck and put them into bottles.

She was also there when they went ashore at Colombo and spent a night of fear on mat beds on the open verandah of a hostel. That day they had watched a fakir entice a brood of cobras out of a basket while he played his flute.

It was an exciting voyage for a group of boys heading to the other end of the earth, but Wilf enjoyed his discoveries about the other boys as much as seeing the sights. "You're lucky to have a father and mother as I was born in an orphanage and never had a father or a mother," one of the boys told Wilf, causing him to reflect on how his life may have varied from other boys his own age. He discovered he was the only Irish boy. Most of the boys were from orphanages around London. Something about the various dialects of English sparked his interest and in a short time he discovered they came from Cornwall, Northumberland, Yorkshire, Lancashire, Manchester, and Birmingham. One boy, Andrew Smeaton, came from Scotland and they shared the same birthday.

As they drew closer to the west coast of Australia, Wilf remembered the colourful brochures his mother and brother had showed him of Australia. But the vision of green grass and blue skies was dashed as the ship approached Fremantle on a miserable wet day. Memories of Southampton returned as they entered a port crowded with ships, wharves, dark buildings, smoke from steamships and locomotives, dark clouds and heavy rain. Before they could get their bearings in this new port, they were on a train to Pinjarra, a tiny Australian community several hours journey southeast of Fremantle.

It was dark and cold and it was starting to dawn on Wilf that there was something more sinister about the trip than what he had originally been told. That perhaps this was a deliberate attempt to take the boys captive. At the Pinjarra Railway Station they were transferred to trucks for an eight-kilometre trip to Fairbridge. He began to take note of where the dusty road was leading, storing up images in his mind of different landmarks so that he could prepare for an escape when he eventually arrived at his destination. He watched carefully as the truck drove through the main gates, then his fears grew as the truck was driven around the village, confirming in his mind that the young passengers were being deliberately confused so they wouldn't know where they were or how to escape.

They pulled up at the front of a wooden cottage. The word "Lawley" was painted on a board near the front door and sixteen of the group were told that this was to be their new home. An officious woman stood by the door of the cottage and watched as Wilf and the other fifteen boys scrambled off the back truck. She introduced herself as Miss Bargh, and told them she was to be their housemother. Still stiff and sore from the ride in the back of the truck and disoriented by the trip, the boys followed her into the jarrah-board building where they were given a big enamel mug full of hot cocoa. Weary and confused they were bundled off to cyclone wire beds for their first night in Australia.

Kingsley Fairbridge and his wife founded the Fairbridge Farm School at Pinjarra, Western Australia, in 1912. After spending the first seventeen years of his life in the seemingly limitless space of Rhodesia, and concerned at the sight of pale-faced, undernourished children in the congested slum areas of England, Fairbridge dreamed of a scheme to transfer these children to a wider, healthier environment. Although his formal education had ended when he was eleven years of age, he returned to Africa and persisted until gaining a Rhodes scholarship in 1909. He dreamed of establishing a farm school in Rhodesia, but was refused land, so when the premier of Western Australia invited him to work in that state, he took the opportunity. Kingsley Fairbridge died in 1924.

When Wilf Douglas and a shipload of boys arrived at Fairbridge five years later, there were over 300 children at the school.

At six o'clock on their first morning, a bugle sounded *Reveille* and Miss Bargh hustled the sixteen new residents of Lawley cottage out of bed and pushed them through a cold shower before directing them to get dressed in khaki shirts and shorts. As the boys tried to get their bearings, they whispered to each other, trying to find the familiar clothes they had been wearing out on the ship. They looked at each other with fear as they realised their luggage had been confiscated, including all the clothing they had brought with them. As an Irish Protestant, Wilf had been taught it was a shame to go barefooted like the Catholic children, so he was shocked when told they were all to learn to go barefooted. It was then time to do their chores.

The boys soon became aware that the range of chores would be a daily responsibility to keep the house running like clockwork. They had to light the kitchen and copper fires, set the table for breakfast, chop the firewood, polish the jarrah floors with crude oil and kerosene, and scrub the linoleum floors in the bathroom and kitchen. After a breakfast of porridge, white bread, dripping and jam, they were required to wash up the breakfast dishes and sweep the dining room floor. Then they would line up to brush their teeth with carbolic powder and water, have their hair, fingernails and knees checked by Miss Bargh. Only then, could they begin the short walk barefoot to school.

5
The Colonel's Eyes

"Well, Douglas, what do you want to be when you grow up?" Fairbridge's Principal, Colonel Heath boomed on Wilf's first day at work.

"An architect, Sir, or an electrical engineer," he quickly replied.

"An architect or an electrical engineer, eh? You'd better work in my gardens for a month," he grunted as he pointed to his small orchard, a poultry run, expansive flower and vegetable gardens, and a woodpile.

It was 6.30 in the morning and already Wilf had been up for an hour and a half supervising the chores of the other fifteen boys in the cottage. He had turned fourteen and had finished primary school, so now after two years at Lawley Cottage he had been appointed a trainee and had been transferred to Glasgow Cottage where he was made cottage leader. He had enjoyed his two years at his new Australian school, both of them in Mr. Bond's class. Mr. Bond was an Englishman who enthralled the boys with stories of his experiences in the war. Although he would occasionally throw a bundle of keys at anyone who wasn't paying attention, he had the ability to make education meaningful and enjoyable for the Irish boy from Lawley Cottage.

Wilf didn't have any influence to apply for a scholarship to attend secondary school, so he was to become a trainee. His first appointment was to work for Colonel Heath. Fairbridge was made up of a large orchard, a herd of dairy cattle, piggeries, sheep, horses, vegetable and flower gardens, an abattoir, and a wood yard. Girls were trained mainly in domestic work, but both boys and girls were given work to do in the main kitchen and in the staff dining room. Fairbridge boys were always in steady demand to work on farms in Western Australia and girls were usually in demand to work as domestics.

In time, he would find himself lecturing in anthropology and linguistics at University, and PhD students would study his ground-breaking work on Aboriginal languages, but at fourteen there was no prospect of secondary education, and he wasn't interested in becoming a farmer, the expected career path for Fairbridge boys.

He looked around the grounds of the principal's residence and recognised the tell-tale signs of a party the previous night. The colonel was known for his parties. He quickly set about cleaning up the mess, clearing away the beer bottles outside the kitchen door and began to carry the dustbin full of leftover sandwiches and cakes to feed the fowls. As he emptied the scraps into the fowl yard he jealously eyed some cake with a thick slab of icing, but before he could rescue it from being thrown to the fowls, the colonel's wife appeared, watching his every move. He watched as the fowls enjoyed the scraps, then as soon as Mrs. Heath disappeared, picked up some of the pieces of icing sugar, washed them and stored them in the shed for later enjoyment.

He was also able to hide a few half empty beer bottles in the shed, and later in the day as the principal headed off on his regular round of the village, Wilf sneaked into the shed and began to drink the warm, flat beer that had been in the open bottles since the previous night. The experience was such that he never drank beer for the rest of his life.

Trenching the chrysanthemum beds was a big job so Colonel Heath arranged for another boy to help Wilf. By midmorning they were tired of digging and decided to go for a walk to the other end of the farm to borrow a mattock to make their work easier. Collecting a mattock wasn't really a two-person job but they wanted the break and agreed they could take turns to carry the mattock back as long as they were careful to get past the house without being noticed. The windows of the colonel's house were like giant eyes. If Wilf made one false move, the colonel or his wife would appear and there would be an order to go on to some other job around the yard. When they were far enough away, they walked leisurely and confidently along one of the middle roads between the cottages. Halfway along the road, they saw Colonel Heath turn into the road ahead of them walking towards them. Without hesitation, the two boys shot through the yard of a nearby cottage and back to the top road and back to the garden. The colonel had long legs, and he reached the top road at the same time as the boys. "Douglas, Come here!" he roared. They stopped in front of him. "Report to me at four o'clock." There was no argument, no explanations. At four o'clock he took the boys to the gravel pit behind his gardens, ordered them to lower their pants, and lathered their naked bottoms with a leather strap.

A chopping block was placed strategically near the back door of Glasgow Cottage. Woodchips were scattered around the ground indicating a spot that was well used. Wilf heaved a heavy branch off his shoulder and placed it on the block and picked up the axe. "How was your day?" Miss Denton asked, as she sidled out the back door and sat down on the rickety wooden step. He put down the axe and told her the whole story. It was good to know that someone would listen. He enjoyed his conversations with her at the woodheap. While most of the housemothers were the matronly type who dressed in sombre clothes, fourteen-year-old Wilf noticed that Miss Denton wore the brightest colours and the shortest dresses. From time to time he would hear the other housemothers remarking on her dress, or the way she walked.

When he knocked off work at five p.m. his first job was to hunt for a log of firewood to take back to the cottage. He would ask the other boys what sort of mood Miss Denton was in, and if she was in a good mood would go straight to her room and tell her about his day and, at times, like today she would sit and watch him chopping the wood. She loved to hear his stories about what had been happening at the principal's house and at Fairbridge House during the day.

Next door to the principal's residence was Fairbridge House, a large two-storey colonial guest house with a shingled roof. Working next door, Wilf had the opportunity to hear the comings and goings of the visitors, and at times when he was required to mow the back lawn of the guest house, would see the gentry sipping tea on the wide, vine-covered verandah of the building. Sometimes a guest would speak to him, but most of the time he was ignored as he carried out his work. Wilf would save up all the stories about the goings-on at the principal's house or Fairbridge House to tell Miss Denton when he returned to Glasgow Cottage after work.

Stories like the time he was reprimanded by a guest for leaving the garden rake on the path. "One of the guests told me a relative had a fractured skull because he had stood on the teeth of a rake and the handle had sprung up and hit him on the head." He told Miss Denton. She smiled as he animatedly described the way the guest had told him off.

They laughed together the day Wilf explained why he had come home with egg yoke dripping down his leg. As he was leaving the principal's gardens, Mrs. Heath called Wilf and gave him a fresh egg for himself. It was the first time she had ever given him anything, so he thanked her, but decided he would give the egg to his Miss Denton. On his way back to Glasgow Cottage, he met a group of boys from the cottage on their way to the river for a swim. He had slipped the egg into his trousers pocket so the boys wouldn't take it off him, but they were intent on getting to the swimming hole and were flicking each other with their towels. When Wilf told them he needed to report to matron, one of the boys cheerfully swiped Wilf with his towel. The friendly swipe cracked the egg in his pocket and its contents trickled down his leg giving him an awkward arrival back at Glasgow Cottage.

As Miss Denton sat on the back step of the cottage watching Wilf chop the wood it was clear that a level of trust had developed between the two. She valued Wilf's leadership of the other boys and enjoyed his stories, and he grasped desperately at the few signs of affection that he could receive from someone who seemed to care for him. But the relationship was not always easy.

On those afternoons when the other boys told Wilf that Miss Denton was "waggy", he would approach her more diplomatically and often with fear because she was quite unpredictable. Sometimes she would be very playful with the boys and at other times would fly into a temper. On one occasion, she swiped the crockery and cutlery off the table in a fit of temper after one of the boys laid the table incorrectly.

One night, the boys went to bed at the usual time of eight p.m., tired but happy. Before settling down they always sang the evening hymn: *Lord keep us safe this night; secure from all our fears; May angels guard us while we sleep; till morning light appears, Amen.* They all slipped off to sleep only to be awoken with a start when Miss Denton, strap in hand, turned on the light and demanded the boys get out of bed. Beginning near the door, she stripped every bed and strapped each occupant, before ordering them into the living room. Standing in their pyjamas, the boys blinked in the light, and shivering with cold and fear, watched as Miss Denton opened the large food cupboard and demanded: "Who spilt that sugar on the shelf? No answer! Alright, Wilfrid Douglas as the leader of this cottage, you will take everything out of this cupboard and wash every shelf. And you boys, will stand there until he's finished!"

Wilf struggled to see any spilt sugar, but as the other boys watched, he laboriously removed everything from the six big shelves, washed them down and waited for them to dry, then replaced everything before they could crawl back to bed wondering what would happen next.

On another evening Miss Denton's mood was very different as she joined the boys in a game of hide and seek. By lights out, the game had turned pretty rowdy. Miss Denton had tipped a small table on its side and was hiding behind it, the boys screaming with delight and knocking chairs out of the way in their attempt to reach Matron. Suddenly the doors of the living room burst open and there stood the head matron, known to everyone as the black beetle, viewing the scene of chaos with a look of unbelief on her face. Then, almost in a scream, she yelled: "Where is your housemother?" A weak voice from behind the upturned table said, "I'm here." Miss Denton stood up and quickly regained her defiant composure. The black beetle was taken aback, but all she could say was, "It's after eight o'clock, Miss Denton, and these boys should be in bed."

When the head matron had gone, Miss Denton told the boys to finish the game more quietly, but quickly threw herself into the fun again as though the regulations did not exist. As the atmosphere became rowdy again, Wilf slipped through the dormitory to the front door and knocked loudly. There was a sudden silence inside and Miss Denton appeared at the door. His joke backfired and the fun was over. Wilf was given a sound scolding, and the boys were sent to bed immediately.

Miss Denton had an uncle who visited her from time to time. He was a surveyor and Matron introduced Wilf to him because he was interested in drawing and architecture. After one of his visits, Miss Denton told Wilf that her uncle was considering taking him on as an apprentice and would like him to draw a plan of Glasgow Cottage as a demonstration of his ability. As soon as possible, with the aid of a ruler, he measured the dimensions of the cottage and eventually produced a scale plan on drawing paper. Strangely, the plan was never presented to the surveyor and the boys never saw him at Fairbridge again. Years later,

Wilf learned that the man was probably not Matron's uncle, but was a boyfriend.

The plans were useful, however, when Miss Denton suggested that together she and Wilf could become landscape artists, and he could draw plans for a new garden layout. The area surrounding Glasgow Cottage was composed mainly of gravel and large gravel stones. Elephant grass and geraniums were the only plants that seemed to grow around the cottage and there was a hedge of elephant grass almost right around the cottage grounds. Miss Denton asked Wilf to make use of the many large stones and boulders lying around the block and to design a large rockery. Of course, once the plan was completed, the young landscape architect was no longer an artist, but one of the workers. At weekends, the inmates of Glasgow worked like slaves, carting stones, sometimes levering them across the yard with crowbars, until they had built a hill almost as high as the cottage itself. Then they carried wheelbarrow loads of soil to fill the cracks and, in time, planted geraniums and other hardy plants all over the rockery. Within a short time, however, the unpredictable Miss Denton wanted the rockery moved to another site, insisting that it was in the wrong place.

During the building of the rockery, there was a distraction when Miss Denton suddenly decided that they needed a tennis court on the east side of the cottage. Over a number of weeks, the sixteen boys with spades, shovels, crowbars, and mattocks changed a fifteen-degree rise into a gravel pit that was never used as a tennis court.

One evening Miss Denton planned a concert at the cottage for the schoolteachers. Wilf knew that this would be important to her, and that he needed to be home on time to help prepare the evening meal. He was just leaving the Colonel's gardens at five o'clock, when the colonel, kerosene bucket in his hand, stopped him and ordered: "Run along to the slaughter yard and get a bucket of blood for my chrysanthemums, Douglas!"

Wilf thought about Miss Denton preparing for her concert and he knew she would be angry if he was late getting home. He also knew that he couldn't disobey an order from the colonel. The eighteen litre kerosene tin had a wire handle, and Wilf struggled back to the colonel with his tin full of blood, desperately hoping that nothing else would be required of him that would delay him any further. Sure enough, the colonel was waiting for him. It was getting late and Wilf suspected that he was already late for the evening meal but the colonel led him off to the chrysanthemum bed and gave instructions about how the blood was to be applied.

Miss Denton was furious when he arrived home. He had missed the evening meal and she wouldn't listen to any excuses. She ordered Wilf to wash the dishes and finish the housework while the boys put on their concert for the schoolteachers. Because of his lateness, the copper boiler hadn't been lit so he began to wash the dishes in lukewarm water. He was already feeling sorry for himself when Miss Denton stormed into the kitchen and asked him why he was washing the dishes in lukewarm water. She smacked him then continued to reprimand him as he lit the copper and waited for the water to heat up ready to continue with the dishes. Finally, the water was hot enough, but by then the concert had started and he could hear the boys trying to entertain the schoolteachers in the living room. He was overwhelmed with self-pity and picked up a table knife out of the sink. Angry at himself and Miss Denton he visciously swiped the knife down on his finger. The knife was blunt and the painful bruise only increased the misery and unfairness of the moment.

He was still feeling sorry for himself as he cleaned up the kitchen and didn't notice Miss Denton slip out of the living room and close the door behind her. The look on her face was very different, as Wilf glanced up from his work and saw her standing demurely in front of him. She pleaded with him: "Douglas, come and do something to save the situation in there. The boys are making fools of themselves. I feel ashamed in front of those teachers. Come and do something to save the evening."

His finger was hurting and Miss Denton's harsh words were still ringing in his ears. Why should he help out someone who had been so unfair? He looked at her for a minute, but her sudden change of demeanour softened him. He went to the bathroom, washed his face and combed his hair, desperately thinking what he could do at short notice. In the bedroom he found a Scottish tartan blanket and threw it over his shoulder. He found a piece of tissue paper and comb, and with the stick that was used for taking the washing out of the copper over the other shoulder, was ready to enter the concert with a hastily constructed set of bagpipes. As he went through his repertoire of Scottish and Irish pipe tunes, which he had heard many times during the Orange processions in Ulster, the headmaster announced the names of the pieces. The final bracket of tunes brought loud applause and Miss Denton sent the rest of the boys to bed and invited him into her private room with the teachers for supper.

Wilf was baptised in the Church of Ireland, but when he got to Fairbridge he was told he would have to be confirmed in the Church of England. He thought that this may be something he should write to his parents about, but was informed this wasn't necessary. "We are your guardians now," he was politely informed. Two Church of England women who Wilf only knew as Little Miss Brown and Big Miss Brown, were assigned to prepare him for baptism and confirmation. Little Miss Brown became the main catechist and also became his godmother. The rector from Pinjarra took Wilf into Fairbridge House, where a small font had been set up. Little Miss Brown took him aside and explained the process, then she presented him to the rector who dipped his finger in the font water, made the sign of the cross on his forehead, and baptised him as Wilfrid Henry Douglas.

The next day, Wilf joined other catechists for confirmation and were taken by truck into the little Church of England in the nearby township of Pinjarra where the Bishop of Bunbury confirmed them. The children went up two by two and the bishop laid his hands on their heads. Wilf was last in the queue, so the bishop laid both his hands on his head and said, "May the Lord bless thee more and more." Then he gave him a text for life, Philippians 3:14, "I press toward the mark for the prize of the high calling of God in Christ Jesus." Wilf had no idea at the time what the text meant, but felt very solemn and determined that he would be a good boy from then onwards.

At the time, there was no proper church building on the farm and the large dining hall was used for church services. While Wilf was working for Colonel Heath, a fine church building was erected and named the Church of the Holy Innocents. On Sundays the "innocents" all dressed in school uniforms, boys wearing the Fairbridge black and yellow striped tie filed into church, cottage by cottage. One of the children had the responsibility of ringing the bell. On his only attempt at doing this task, Wilf was lifted off his feet by the weight of the bell, and was never given another chance to ring the bell. Wilf often said this was the most uplifting experience he ever had in the Church of the Holy Innocents.

****

The Church of the Holy Innocents, Fairbridge

As Wilf was chopping wood for the colonel's wood box, a trench digger hanging on the wall of the shed fell on his head. The sharp end of the tool opened up the flesh on the top of his skull and the blood began running down his face. Anxious not to let anyone see his injuries, Wilf picked up his soft khaki hat, pressed it firmly on the wound with both hands and began to walk to the hospital. As he passed the rectory, the new chaplain, Reverend Charles Challen, called out: "Is that all you've got to do, boy? Pull yourself together, walk straight and swing those arms!"

Wilf blurted out in reply, "The blood's running out, sir!" He had to repeat his reply a couple of times before the chaplain caught on to the seriousness of the situation and shouted: "Wait there, boy." He ran down the path to where Wilf was standing, lifted his khaki hat and examined the wound, then keen to get him to the hospital as soon as possible, hurried along with Wilf and explained the situation to the matron who cleaned up the blood-matted hair and patched up the wound.

It wasn't long before Wilf appeared before Reverend Challen again, but this time to receive his farewell instructions before leaving Fairbridge. The move came unexpectedly. His traineeship had apparently been completed and someone had decided that it was time for young Wilf to find his place in the world. "Be sure you have something worthwhile to do in your spare time," Reverend Challen advised the young teenager, when he was called to the main office and told the date of his departure from Fairbridge. The staff issued him with a suitcase containing work clothes, boots, underclothes, pyjamas, towels and a good shirt and tie, and shorts.

The Glasgow Cottage boys gave him a send-off breakfast on the day he left the farm. No special food, only much joking and the assurance that they would save his evening meal for him as they were sure he would be back again by then. Wilf's mind was made up. He was determined never to return to Fairbridge again as an inmate. He was taken by truck to the railway station at Pinjarra and was told to alight at a place called Kelmscott, an outer suburb of Perth, and then to report for duty to Major General Whittingham. It was with mixed feelings he travelled on that train—once again, a lonely Irish boy in Australia with an unknown future ahead.

6
Lessons in Nyungar

It had been a tiring day for Bob Mead. He had been fox hunting all day and was walking along a dusty road towards his home at Badjaling. Foxes were an introduced species, and they caused a lot of trouble to the farmers who worked in the area, so Bob found some satisfaction in proving his hunting skills and at the same time collecting a small payment from the white farmers who hired him. The Nyungar people were barely recognised by the farmers, but they were considered useful when it came to getting rid of pests like foxes.

As he made his way to Badjaling, with a bundle of fox carcasses dragging behind him, Bob spotted the new school teacher. He was a young man, only twenty-one years of age, but already going bald at the front. They chatted for a while about the fox hunting expedition, then, with a twinkle in his eye the Nyungar elder said: "Mr Douglas, say *ngangk*!" The young Irishman had been told that the Badjaling people only spoke English; this was his first realisation that while English was used widely, there was something about these people that he had yet to learn.

His first attempt at repeating the word wasn't too successful, so Bob called over his seven-year-old son Aubrey, one of the thirty-eight children who attended the tiny corrugated iron school now in the hands of this young teacher. Aubrey screwed up his nose and said, "ngangk." The teacher screwed up his nose and tried again to repeat the word.

"When you can say that word, I'll teach you another one," Bob said. "Ngangk is our Nyungar word for mother, and it's also the word for the sun in the sky because the sun is the mother of us all." Wilf Douglas had received his first lesson in both the Nyungar language and traditional Nyungar beliefs.

Bob taught Wilf another important cultural lesson in his first month at Badjaling. Wilf was visiting the camps and saw the mission hammer on the cleared ground near the fireplace at the front of Bob Mead's camp. He recalled that Miss Belshaw had told him that someone had borrowed the mission hammer and had not returned it, so he picked up the hammer and took it back to the mission house. About dark, Bob came back from hunting, went straight to Wilf's house and called him out.

"Mr. Douglas, you are guilty of stealing property from my home."

Wilf thought he was joking, and explained that he just picked up the hammer that was lying on the ground and brought it back to the mission house where it belonged. Bob wasn't joking. He made it clear that a serious crime had been committed by going into someone's home without permission and removing an article without telling the owner. Wilf quickly learned that what he thought was only a cleared place on the ground was really someone's home and should be respected as such.

After Bob's initial language lesson, Wilf began learning more words and delighted the people by using them whenever possible. The young men would sometimes visit the mission house to play board games and Wilf would take the opportunity to practice his new language skills. Not only was he keen to learn, the Badjaling people were keen teachers.

Granny McKay was visiting one day and as she sat Wilf on the edge of the verandah made out of railway sleepers, she began teaching him the Nyungar words for the parts of the body. When she came to the word for tongue, Wilf thought she said "darling", so repeated "darling." But she corrected him and said, "No, *d'arlin'*."

The young language student said darling again and she corrected him again with d'arlin', helping Wilf to see that he needed to put his tongue between his teeth for the "d" and "n" to vocalise what he would discover many years later were interdental sounds. The pair suddenly realised that Miss Belshaw was standing at the door nearly splitting her sides laughing as she thought the old Nyungar matron and the young school teacher were calling each other darling.

This tiny Aboriginal community in the Western Australian wheatbelt was at last a place that Wilf Douglas could call home. Not only had he found a family, he was beginning to get an inkling of his purpose in life. A young man who had not attended high school and was not trained as a teacher spent three years teaching children whom he grew to consider as members of his family.

It was from Badjaling that Wilf was called up for military service, so it was to this new-found home that he would return whenever he had leave. Then, after a few years missionary service in another Great Southern wheatbelt town he would eventually return to Badjaling with his new wife before entering into another exciting stage in life.

***

Life in Badjaling seemed a world away from Fairbridge, yet only a handful of years had passed from the day this young Irish teenager boarded a train, glad to be leaving an institution that had defined his life up to that point, but with an uncertain future with no family, no friends, and no direction.

Not surprisingly, there was no one to meet Wilf when the train from Pinjarra to Perth stopped at the empty Kelmscott platform. He found the stationmaster, gave him his ticket, and asked where he could find Major General Whittingham's place.

"Go down this road to a bush track, where you'll find a little bridge over the river. At the top of the track you'll find Whittingham's orchard and home on one side of the road, and their poultry farm on the other," he was told.

Knocking at the scullery door at the back of the house he could hear the voices of two women talking over each other.

"Is that your suitcase, Queenie? ... But, Queenie, that's not your case." One of the women appeared at the door:

"Why did you bring that suitcase here? Who gave you that suitcase? Did Mr. Whittingham tell you to bring that suitcase here?" Mrs. Whittingham noticed the boy at the door was holding a letter.

"Oh, so Mr. Arnott has sent a note, has he?"

"Goodness gracious, NO! You're not the boy from Fairbridge are you? Imagine them sending a boy like this. Goodness me, he can hardly carry his suitcase. Put it down, boy, but don't change your clothes or anything. I'm sure my husband will send you back, you're so small."

After a brief explanation to her sister, Queenie, Mrs. Whittingham pointed from the back door to a small shed nearby.

"That's your room over there. Go and put down your suitcase; but wait until my husband comes home. I'm sure he'll send you back to Fairbridge."

Sitting on the edge of a fold-up stretcher bed he looked around the tiny corrugated iron shed. There was a wooden kerosene box at the head of the stretcher with a hurricane lantern and a box of matches. Other than this and the concrete floor and tiny louvered window, the main feature of the shed was two big chicken incubators. Even Fairbridge was better than this, he thought.

A loud military voice disturbed his thoughts: "Boy, where are you?"

"Here sir!" he replied and left the shed quickly to see an ageing Major General with a long cigarette-holder in his mouth.

"Boy, do you know what elephant grass looks like?"

Recollecting the elephant grass that surrounded Glasgow Cottage he responded confidently. "Yes sir!"

"Well, do you know what couch grass looks like?"

"Yes sir!"

Once again, he recalled his efforts to eradicate the tough couch grass from Colonel Heath's garden.

"Well, juldee, boy! Go and get the couch grass out of the elephant grass patch!"

Wilf was to learn in time that Bert Whittingham had brought the word *juldee* from India where he had used it frequently to hurry up his Indian servant boys.

The slight teenager from Fairbridge knew how to work hard and was determined that Mr. Whittingham wouldn't send him back there. By the time the major general came to see how he was progressing, the patch of couch grass had nearly gone.

"Well, leave that, boy, and come with me."

Taking Wilf to the poultry farm he explained his duties. He would rise at six a.m. to milk the two cows, mix the mash of green chaff, meat-meal, bone-meal, pollard and bran for the fowls, then to take the food over to the poultry and distribute it in the various pens. Later in the day he would take a sickle and cut an armload of elephant grass or lucerne and put it through the hand-operated chaff cutter to be ready in the mixing bath for next morning's "mash." The afternoon ration for the fowls was wheat and green feed. The eggs had to be collected and taken to the house where Mrs. Whittingham weighed them for grading and packing for market.

Mr. Whittingham had his poultry and orchard very well organised. The fowl pens were large and clean. The hens were in big yards that had been ploughed and sown with oats, barley or lucerne. When the green feed had been cut down and used in the mash, the fowls were let loose in the clean yard, then the yard in which they had previously been was ploughed and sown. The laying fowls were locked up in large, airy sheds at night. Their perches were kept clean and, from time to time, were sprayed with methylated spirits that was ignited to burn out any lice or stick fast fleas. As well as the six or more yards for the laying fowls and roosters, there was a large natural bush enclosure for turkeys. Wilf was later to discover that it would be his task at times to chop off the turkeys' heads and pluck them ready for sale.

At dinnertime on that first day, Wilf was invited into the kitchen of the house and Mrs. Whittingham introduced him to Sybil, the housekeeper. She was a buxom country girl, and he learned that Sybil and he had to eat in the kitchen while the Whittinghams dined in style in the large dining room. When anything was required, Mrs. Whittingham would tinkle a small bell and Sybil would jump to attend to her.

The Whittinghams seemed to have plenty to talk about, especially as Queenie had just arrived from England for a brief visit, but Wilf was rather shy about talking to Sybil and was not sure that talking would be allowed in the kitchen. Sybil spoke in a quiet voice and asked about

Fairbridge and the trip from Pinjarra. She proved to be very friendly and tried to make him feel at home.

Mrs. Whittingham leaned back in her chair in the dining room and looked out into the kitchen. "Sybil!" she called in a tentative sort of voice as she held a delicate china cup between her finger and thumb. "Is this my Hangmee tea?" she asked.

"Yes, Mrs. Whittingham," replied Sybil.

"I thought it was a nice cup of tea," she commented.

Sybil turned to Wilf and whispered, "I gave her Bushells tonight!" At that point, he concluded that Sybil and he would get along fine. Nevertheless, his first night out in the incubator house was a very lonely one but he was very tired, too, so soon dropped off to sleep. His last thought as he drifted off was one of satisfaction that he had not been sent back to Fairbridge.

At breakfast time, they all ate at the same table in the kitchen. This arrangement gave Mr. Whittingham the opportunity to tell Wilf and Sybil about his life at sea and in India. Bert Whittingham had been a merchant seaman; a pilot in the port of Calcutta, taking ships up the Hooghly River at high tide, and a major general in the Indian Army. Helen Whittingham claimed to be the first British nurse to cross the English Channel by aircraft during World War I. They had no children.

Mrs. Whittingham often talked about her health and why she had to eat two rice puddings each day. She was very particular about how the rice puddings were cooked, so she insisted on cooking them herself. On one occasion, though, she must have forgotten that her rice pudding was in the oven and when she smelt something burning she rushed with an oven cloth, took the smoking pudding out of the oven and flung it out onto the cement floor of the scullery. It was a miracle the hot dish and the splattering rice didn't hit Sybil, who had to clean up the mess.

A couple of days later, Wilf overheard Mrs. Whittingham chastising Sybil:
"I notice there is a chip off my pudding dish, Sybil. You'll have to be more careful with it in future." Sybil didn't say a word.

Wilf had the opportunity to tell Mrs. Whittingham that his ambition was to become an architect or an electrical engineer. She reminded him that to qualify for either of these vocations he would need to study mathematics. So saying, she went to her room and brought out two books, one on Euclid and the other on algebra, and recommended that he work his way through both books and do the exercises. This task occupied Wilf for many evenings, and he discovered that he was mentally stimulated by the exercises. A local doctor, learning from Mrs. Whittingham that her boy was using a piece of cardboard as a compass to do the exercises in geometry, gave him a solid silver compass set.

In time, without a tutor, he got tired of mathematics and gradually replaced these studies with the reading of Mr. Whittingham's library books. These books were brought from Boans department store in Perth each fortnight, along with Mrs. Whittingham's grocery order, and while Mr. Whittingham was reading the previous set, Wilf would read the new lot by lantern light at night in his incubator shed.

The time came when the two big incubators were filled with fertile eggs. Wilf's task was to see that the kerosene heaters maintained a constant temperature. When the chickens began to emerge, he was transferred from the shed to the verandah of the main house. The floor was cleared in the shed and the kerosene-heated brooders were placed on the floor ready to act as mothers for the newly hatched chicks. After the chicks were hatched, they were either sold or placed in the poultry farm until they became young pullets and began laying eggs themselves. When he had cleaned the shed, he moved back again with his stretcher and box and lantern.

Some of the young pullets on one occasion were allowed to run loose in the orchard after it had been ploughed. Wilf was standing outside the scullery door talking to Sybil. She had asked if he liked playing cricket, and he explained that since he had been run over by an armoured car in Belfast, he found it difficult to bowl overarm. He picked up a stone and swung his arm to demonstrate his disability. The stone flew from his hand, but at that moment, some young pullets ran from behind a tree right in the path of the stone. One of the pullets fell over and lay squawking on the ground. Wilf ran to it immediately and found that its leg had been broken. His only thought was to conceal the evidence, so with the support of Sybil, he decapitated the pullet and buried it under a tree in the orchard, but his conscience troubled him so much he went to Mrs. Whittingham and confessed.

"Why on earth did you bury it?" she exclaimed. "I could have had it for my tea. Go and dig it up again and bring it here!"

When Wilf brought the exhumed body to her, she gasped, "Phew! I couldn't eat that. Go and bury it again!" So he carried out a reburial ritual with a clear conscience.

The Whittinghams had a large Airdale dog and a Hillman car. When they went out in the car, or even if Mr. Whittingham moved it in the yard, the Airdale was locked up in the house. He never learned that it was dangerous to get in the way of the motor car. Mrs. Whittingham decided that Sandy, the dog, needed to have a run, so asked Wilf to take a letter to the post office in the main street and take Sandy with him. He went on his bicycle down the lane, over the little bridge, and through the bush to the Albany Road. It was about a kilometre farther on to the post office, riding the bicycle along the left side of the road and Sandy running alongside his left. They had barely gone a few bicycle lengths when a driver came behind the two of them in a Hillman car and tooted his horn. Hearing a horn that sounded the same as the car his boss drove, Sandy excitedly ran out in front of the Hillman and was hit on the back of the head. The car didn't stop and Sandy ran to the side of the road and collapsed. Wilf rushed across to him and found a tiny trickle of blood running from his mouth. The dog was dead.

Wilf was shocked and worried. He rode his bike back to the house, told Sybil the bad news as he went through the scullery, learned that Mrs. Whittingham was outside somewhere, and broke down and cried at the kitchen door. A few minutes later, Mrs. Whittingham walked into the house. When she saw him crying brokenheartedly, she blurted out to Sybil: "What's wrong with him? Has his mother died or something?" When Sybil explained the situation, she screamed, caught hold of Wilf and cried out: "I'll never forgive you for this! I'll never forgive you for this! Never! Never! Never!"

At this moment, Mr. Whittingham appeared and asked what was wrong. When he heard the news, he calmly said: "Come along, boy, and show me where he is." They walked to where Sandy was lying under a bush near the roadside. They had brought a sack with them, so Mr. Whittingham said: "Put him in the sack, boy, and let us take him back to the house."

It was a terrible day and a sad funeral. After it was over, Mrs. Whittingham announced that there was only one condition on which she would forgive him: that was if he were to go to the hills, find a nice white stone, and carve Sandy's name on it. Wilf went out the following weekend, found a suitable stone and managed, with a cold chisel, to carve the name, "Sandy".

7
The Lone Scout

There was a buzz in the audience as the crowd moved to find their place on the hard wooden seats laid out neatly in rows in the Kelmscott Hall. There wasn't much entertainment in town, so the regular concerts organised by the local Lone Scout group at the small wooden-framed hall were popular, and particularly as word had gotten around about a new conjuring act. The teenager had recently joined the Lone Scouts and had started to attract some interest at the concerts. He had learned some tricks in Belfast as a boy where he used to trade foreign stamps for trick equipment and had begun to build up a store of trick equipment since moving to Kelmscott from Fairbridge.

One of Wilf's favourites involved getting a member of the audience to place a pocket watch in a small black bag. However, on this occasion there appeared to be only one rather wary man who had a pocket watch. As he placed his watch in the bag and tied the drawstring at the top, he warned the young conjuror to be very careful as the watch had special sentimental value. Wilf walked up to the table, showed the audience an empty black box and placed the bag in the box. After some show business talk, he lifted out a black bag and threw it on the floor. There was the sound of metal and glass breaking, then to the consternation of the volunteer from the audience, he jumped on the bag, thoroughly destroying its contents.

By this time the owner of the watch was on his feet shouting all sorts of abuse and threats at the young conjuror. Apologetically Wilf picked up the bag, lit a candle and burned what was left of the bag. Then, apologising for making such a mess of the fellow's watch, he walked over to him and presented him with a small box covered in gift wrapping and tied with a ribbon, saying that he hoped it would compensate for his loss. It was a nervous moment for the audience since the man did not want any substitute and threatened to take the Lone Scout to court, even threatening physical injury. It was only the restraining influence of the good-natured audience that saved the situation.

In the end, Wilf had to assure him it was only a trick and if he were to open the package he would find his watch intact. Others helped him rip open the package and open the little black bag. Even when he held the watch in his hand, he still threatened that if he did not find the inscription on the inside of the back, he would take the conjurer to court. He had so lost face by the time he opened the watch and checked the inscription that he retreated from the hall amidst the cheering and booing of the audience.

The original box had a diagonal division inside and the bag that Wilf jumped on and burnt was a second bag that contained an old watch. The original black bag with the man's watch in it had been dropped into the separate division of the box and was slipped through a gap in the box into the gift-wrapped box.

***

Because Wilf painted the signs and prepared the handouts for the Boy Scout concerts, other organisations began calling on him to do ticket writing. Before long he was painting notices for the Church of England fancy dress ball and other social attractions in the district. With the three shillings and ninepence a week he was earning at the Whittinghams, plus the little he gained from ticket writing, in time he was able to buy an English bicycle with an acetylene gas headlamp and brake.

The Whittinghams gave Wilf most Saturday and Sunday afternoons off except when they wanted to go somewhere and leave him to feed the fowls, milk the cows, and do the other essential jobs. When he had time off, he cycled around the district. He visited Sybil's home on the Roleystone Road and met her mother and father and her young sister, Maisie. He also pedaled along the Albany Road sometimes in the Perth direction as far as Maddington or Cannington, or southwards to Armadale. On one trip he found another Fairbridge boy, Tommy Langford, who worked on Maffescioni's vineyard near Cannington. After that meeting, Tommy used to visit Wilf some weekends and bring him a bottle of Maffescioni's best wine that he kept behind the incubator shed door for use during the week.

Patrick O'Connell was another Fairbridge boy who lived fairly close to Kelmscott and through him, met a boy by the name of Stanley who had been a great friend at Fairbridge. He had been a member of the "Invention Department" and helped produce a magazine for their schoolmates who were interested in space travel and new inventions. Stanley had changed. He was more worldly-wise than Wilf and scorned the kind of life he was living at Whittinghams and in the Boy Scout group. He proudly claimed to be a Scout Master himself and told Wilf about the dances and free concerts they could attend and urged him to visit the Perth brothels with them and other places where he could have his eyes opened to the pleasures of the world. He was tempted, but his conscience wouldn't allow him to accept their invitations. On one or two occasions, Wilf went to the dances in Armadale, but felt a misfit in this environment so took to cycling longer distances when he had time off from work.

There was another place where Wilf soon realised he didn't belong. He used to go to church with Mrs. Whittingham on the Sunday mornings when he was free. The services were run strictly according to the prayer book and were attended mainly by elderly women. Mrs. Whittingham criticised the hats of the women and complained about the squeaky organ. One Sunday, on the way back to the house, she declared, "When I win charities I will buy a new organ for the church." A week or so later, as Wilf held a sick fowl so she could paint its throat with iodine, she passed a remark about one of the rings on her finger. "When I win Tattersalls," she said, "I will buy a diamond sapphire ring for myself."

"But," Wilf interjected, "you said you would buy a new organ for the church if you won, Mrs. Whittingham." She took the spatula out of the hen's beak and referring to the different results that can be achieved from public and private lotteries, she retorted: "That was only if I won charities. That's only two thousand pounds. That wouldn't be enough for a diamond sapphire ring. Tattersalls is 20,000 pounds!"

Mr. Whittingham did not like his wife visiting the fowl yards to look for sick birds. When he accompanied Wilf to the poultry run, if he spotted any sick-looking fowl, he would tell him to catch, kill and bury it, then would issue the warning: "Not a word to the wife about this, boy!" He would give him the same warning if a turkey-hen got out and he knocked it unconscious while trying to drive it back into its yard with a big stick.

***

Wilf was very lonely and seldom heard from home, so demanded more affection from Sybil than necessary. One Sunday night he waited for Sybil to return from her weekend at home and told her he couldn't go to bed until she arrived, as he was so lonely. She gave him a kiss and told him to go to bed. The lone scout returned to his incubator shed thankful for Sybil's caring attitude, but was longing for home and family. He remembered his mother, father and brother Woodrow. His mother was unable to write because of her paralysis. He recalled the times they used to go to Tandragee when he and his brother would play with Annie Maginnis in the hayloft. Then cousin Esmee came to mind. She had been teaching him to play the piano, and she was the one who gave him the New Testament. Wilf felt around in the bottom of the suitcase under his bed and found the little Testament. Opening it, he read the words on the flyleaf: "To Wilfrid, to remind you of your promise to write. Love, Esmee."

So Esmee loved me, he thought. Wasn't that beautiful? He turned the page and began reading the first chapter of St. Matthew. "...Abraham begat Isaac; and Isaac begat Jacob; and Jacob begat Judas and his brethren; and Judas begat Phares and Zara of Thamar...." In a short time, sleep had overcome him. He awoke in the night to find the hurricane lantern still burning and, unaffected by what he had read, put the New Testament back at the bottom of his suitcase.

***

It was Good Friday 1936, and Wilf, now eighteen-years-old was sitting in a bus with an old Fairbridge friend who worked nearby. Somehow some dramatic changes had occurred in a couple of years since he stuffed the New Testament at the bottom of the suitcase, because he and his friend were heading to Victoria Park to attend church. He had been at the Whittinghams for three years when an opportunity came to change his employment, so he was now working at an orchard in Gosnells. Mr. Gordon was a Scotsman who was a guard on the railways and his wife, a non-practising Roman Catholic, directed activities in the house and on the orchard. There were a couple of cows to milk and a plough horse to care for.

As the bus carried them along Albany Road, he looked out and saw a tree that had set him off on a journey of discovery. The bus continued on its way, but Wilf's mind was still back at the tree and what had happened since then. He chuckled at the thought he was now on his way to church. During one of his many long bike rides along that road he had seen a sign on a tree advertising a lecture on the subject of the great pyramid of Giza to be given by a representative of the British Israel World Foundation. At the Whittinghams, his view of Christianity had developed into a cynical opposition to institutionalised Anglicanism, encouraged by his experiences at the Fairbridge church and from listening to Mrs. Whittingham's views on Christianity. He expressed his cynicism and sarcasm about the church to Sybil's younger sister on one of her few visits to the Whittinghams, then regretted having done so later. He was really scared of God and tried to say his prayers every night in case the end of the world should come before morning.

There was something about the advertisement on the tree that caught his attention and it didn't take long for him to become fascinated by the charts of the pyramid and their teaching that World War I, the economic depression, the second coming of Christ and many other important events were clearly predicted by the pyramid measurements.

As the bus continued down Albany Road, Wilf looked out the window at the various landmarks that had become familiar to him during his bike rides recalling that he had become an ardent evangelist for British Israelitism until the day Tommy Langford came to see him, this time without his usual bottle of Maffescioni's wine. Instead, he asked him what day he kept for worship, so at Tommy's invitation, he had begun attending the local Seventh Day Adventist Church where the charts of the pyramid were replaced by graphic pictures of the Antichrist, the woman robed in scarlet, the mark of the Beast, and the Papal crown. Out of fear, he had followed their teaching and told the Whittinghams he could no longer work on Saturday, but would be prepared to work for them on Sunday.

The bus stopped at Victoria Park and he and his friend got off and began walking to the Church of Christ hoping to attend a Good Friday service. After attending the church for a while, he had assumed that Good Friday would be celebrated, not appreciating that among other unusual practices, this particular church had made a decision not to recognize the day. The local policeman had invited Wilf there originally and although he was still attending the Seventh Day Adventist Church on Saturday, and was investigating spiritualism and Russelism (later known as Jehovah's Witnesses), he had accepted the invitation. On his first visit, an appeal was made to come to the front of the church to become a Christian. He was confused about the challenge, but decided he would follow the call the following Sunday.

The policeman, a member of the church, said that he hadn't intended to go the next week, but when Wilf told him he had decided to go up to the front when the appeal for salvation was made, he gruffly replied, "Well, I'll take you, but you'd better step out or I'll be angry with you... it will be a waste of petrol to take you seventeen miles for nothing!" Obediently, Wilf responded to the preacher's invitation that night and was told to come back the following week to be baptised. No one counselled him, although he was crying out in his heart to be put right with God.

He continued to try to keep the Saturday Sabbath and attend the Sunday night services in Victoria Park, was baptised by immersion by a man who reprimanded him for not putting his handkerchief to his nose as he lowered him backwards into the water, and later, was received into membership of the church with no assurance that his sins were forgiven.

Finally, Wilf and his friend arrived at the church only to find that it was closed. They waited until nearly midday, but when no one came, they checked the address of the secretary on the notice board, and set off to find out what time the Good Friday meeting would be held. They did not know the streets of this Perth suburb and weren't used to walking on pavements so, by the time they reached the address, it was nearly five o'clock in the afternoon and they were very tired, hot and hungry. The secretary was mowing his lawn and treated them offhandedly, explaining that his church didn't observe Good Friday. He did not offer them a drink or a rest, but continued to mow his lawn.

Wilf and his friend walked away, resolving not to have anything to do with Christianity again. They were disgusted as well as tired and hungry and trudged the long distance back to the Albany Road again and caught the first bus that came along. It was crowded with holidaymakers returning home, so they found separate seats near the back of the bus. Wilf's friend sat behind him, beside an old Irishman from Kelmscott.

After a while the old man leaned over the back of Wilf's seat and said in a loud County Tyrone dialect, "Oi'm jolly pleased to know you're a Christian." Wilf was embarrassed as the people in the bus looked around to see what a Christian looked like. Then he leaned over again and in a loud whisper said, "You're welcome to come to John Gilchrist's place anytime you loik." It occurred to Wilf that here was a chance to avoid returning to Gordon's for the evening where he would be expected to milk the cows. After a short hesitation he accepted the invitation, and the old man leaned forward again and said, "Yes, come! And you're right welcome."

Contact with this eighty-six-year-old man led to the turning point in Wilf's life. At first, he was very wary because, when he entered his little cottage in Kelmscott, he handed the teenager a Christian newspaper entitled, *The Christian Herald*. After he had started up his Primus stove and put a couple of eggs on to boil, he sat down beside him and said, "Man, it's not baptism will save you. Man, if baptism could save you there would have been no need for Jesus Christ to have come down and die for you." At this point he hurried to the kitchen to attend to the eggs and the bread and butter.

On his return with two boiled eggs and two slices of bread and butter, John Gilchrist continued his message making it clear to Wilf that all his "righteousnesses were as filthy rags", that his salvation depended on "the finished work of Christ on the Cross" and that it was not by trying to do good, but by trusting in Jesus that he would be saved.

Week by week, Wilf visited Mr. Gilchrist and listened to his exposition of Scripture, from Genesis to Revelation and at Mr. Gilchrist's requests, would read aloud many of the sermons of the 19th century Baptist preacher, Charles Haddon Spurgeon. One free afternoon, back at Gordon's place, Wilf knelt on the concrete verandah and recounted to the Lord all he had been doing to please him, then made the definite decision that all his good works were as filthy rags and mentally threw them away. He told the Lord that he was accepting Jesus Christ as his Saviour and Lord and thanked him for taking his place and dying for him on the Cross.

That night he cycled to John Gilchrist's cottage in Kelmscott and told his friend that he had put his trust in the Lord Jesus. The old man looked around for something he could kneel on, "in case you dirty your pants on the floor." Then he said, "Now kneel down, brother, and thank the Lord for what He's done for you." Wilf knelt down, put his head on his hands and began to pray. Without warning, Old John exclaimed, "Stop man! Who are you talking to?"

Wilf replied, "To the Lord."

"Well man", he rejoined, "don't be talking to the devil. Where's the Lord?"

When Wilf replied that he was up in heaven, he looked at him with a beaming smile on his face and said, "Well, then, lift up your head and talk to the Lord, man. You've got nothing to be ashamed of now. Jesus is your righteousness, so you can talk to the Father boldly. You're his son now."

When Wilf told Mrs. Gordon he had become a Christian, she told him that, although she was then a Roman Catholic, she had once been in the Salvation Army, and encouraged him to join the Christian Endeavour group at the local Methodist Church as he would need the support of other Christians. Although she seemed pleased that he had become a Christian, she also became very critical of him and picked him for every little action that she deemed un-Christian. Her husband was a dour Scottish non-church-going Presbyterian who took no notice of him as long as he did the work on the orchard.

Wilf found the little Methodist Church and joined the Senior Christian Endeavour Society and attended the church services. Reverend Victor Deakin was the minister and he quickly pushed Wilf into writing papers for the Christian Endeavour meetings, to help in the Sunday school and even called on him to preach from the pulpit.

It was at the Endeavour meeting that Wilf met Edna. They became attracted to each other and one night he walked home with her. As they stood at her back door in the moonlight, the situation was so romantic they dared to kiss each other. Wilf thought this was the end of his loneliness and for a few weeks they would go for walks together when they were free. Wilf talked about being a missionary and going out by faith to preach the gospel, maybe to China. But this proved to be too much for Edna and the romance ended.

Wilf had read the book, *Pastor Hsi* by Mrs. Howard Taylor of the China Inland Mission and wanted to go to China straight away to preach the gospel. John Gilchrist urged him to go to Perth Bible Institute (PBI) to study. He had been instrumental in leading another Belfast man, Wilson Brown, to Christ and he had gone to PBI and later entered the Baptist ministry. Wilf, just nineteen, wrote to the Institute and received a kindly letter from its founder, Rev. Carment Urquhart who recommended that he should do the correspondence lessons for the rest of the year then consider entering the Institute full-time the following year.

Wilf found correspondence lectures very difficult to do at the Gordons' place. Mr. Gordon's Scottish nature demanded that he should not use the electric light in his bedroom, so he had to study in the living room where Mr. and Mrs. Gordon sat listening to the wireless every evening. As he battled with names like Clement of Rome, Tertullian of Carthage, Justin Martyr and Polycarp and the evidences they presented as to the authenticity of Christianity, Wilf determined that he must go to the institute as a full-time student. When he told Mrs. Gordon, she seemed quite happy about the idea, but when she realised he would have to leave her employ, she told him to leave immediately. She handed him two shillings and sixpence and told him that was all that was due to him as she had to buy clothes for him while he was working for them.

Wilf attended the Kalamunda Christian Convention where he learned something about trusting God to supply his needs. When the offering was taken up, he put his hand into his pocket and only managed to grasp a two-shilling piece when the offering plate reached him. He realised that the sixpence was all he had to enter the Bible Institute, but believed he had given the money to the Lord and told him to keep it. After the meeting, a new-found friend came and shook hands with Wilf, simultaneously squeezing in his hand two, two-shilling pieces—double what he had just put into the offering plate!

A letter from the principal of the Institute contained the offer of free board and a few shillings a week if he would be willing to work for the housemother at the college for the first term. Wilf accepted this offer as another provision of God and entered Perth Bible Institute at the beginning of 1937.

8
Down the Line to Badjaling

The door swung open to the young man who was standing on the wide verandah with his suitcase. The housemother of Perth Bible Institute, Mrs. Naomi Dobbie invited Wilf into the passage of the large bungalow situated on a long sandy-soil block of land in the northern Perth suburb of Joondana Heights. As quickly as she had opened the door she disappeared and the young man was left standing while she went to speak to her one hundred-year-old mother. After a moment standing alone, she hurried back to ask the visitor if he knew anything about wireless sets. Amused that this was the first question he was asked at a Bible Institute, he replied that he had tinkered with crystal sets as a boy. At that, she told him to fix her crystal set and get the cricket scores for her as she must hurry out to do her shopping.

While shocked by his unexpected welcome, it was no challenge to get back to his boyhood hobby of making crystal sets. It was a simple matter to straighten the cat's whisker and to pick up a wireless station. He was not very interested in cricket, and apparently Mrs. Dobbie was not interested either because she ignored the piece of paper Wilf handed her containing the cricket scores. She took him outside and explained that he must have a bed under the house as the main building accommodation was for the women students.

That night, another male student, Lloyd Tranter, and Wilf slept on cyclone beds underneath the high-stumped floor of the girls' quarters. Next day they discovered that the building was composed of a kitchen, a dining room, which was also the lecture room, private rooms for Mrs. Dobbie and her aged mother, and a dormitory-style section for the girls.

Wilf was captivated by the lectures given by Rev. Carment Urquhart, the founder and principal of the college and leaned forward to listen to the principal as he presented lectures in a quiet but authoritative voice on Old and New Testament books, Greek New Testament and Bible doctrine. Every so often Mr. Urquhart's voice would crack as he raised his voice to drive a point home, and it wasn't unusual for the lectures to be interrupted by the sound of Mrs. Dobbie clattering the dishes in the adjoining kitchen. A falling saucepan would be followed by Mrs. Dobbie's voice exclaiming "Praise the Lord" in a tone that sounded more like an expletive than a statement of worship.

Mrs. Dobbie enjoyed the principal's lectures as much as the students and would often make use of a double-sided cupboard that separated the kitchen from the lecture room, in order to hear his talks better. Wilf smiled as he listened to the principal's devotional address to start the new day's activities because he could hear Mrs. Dobbie opening the cupboard door on the kitchen side of the cupboard. At her request he had already opened the cupboard door on the lecture room side of the cupboard so that she could hear the devotional talk. Standing in the kitchen she put her head right inside the cupboard in order to hear the message more clearly, then halfway through Mr. Urquhart's talk, there was a loud explosion in the cupboard, a shocked scream from Mrs. Dobbie and a clatter of crockery as her head hit the shelf. A yeast bottle had blown its cork!

Speakers' class was not always as inspiring as Mr. Urquhart's talks. For this subject, students had to prepare a sermon and deliver it in front of the other students with the Reverend Edward Hogg, a Baptist pastor, acting as chairman and adjudicator. One of the girl students, sometimes referred to as "Little Miss Weir", and who was later to become Mrs. Douglas, described one of Wilf's sermon deliveries as being like "a fast goods train which stops briefly from time to time to drop off goods."

For the first term he scrubbed floors and washed pots for Mrs. Dobbie, but other arrangements were made for house-help in second term, so he had to find some way to earn his weekly board money. He mowed lawns in the wealthy part of Mount Lawley with the owners' hand mowers, and with the money he earned bought a secondhand bicycle and started ticket-writing, the painting of hand-lettered signs most commonly used by shops to promote their goods. With little money to spare, he went into Clarksons in Perth and ordered poster colours, brushes and pasteboard. The shop assistant asked how much money he had to spend, and when he was told "twelve shillings and sixpence," looked at the young man and said, "are you from the Bible Institute?" When Wilf replied affirmatively, he told him that he also was a Christian and that he could select more useful items than he had chosen and they would not cost so much. For Wilf's twelve shillings and sixpence he acquired a set of the best pre-war sable hair ticket-writer's brushes and enough card to meet orders for the next few weeks.

Delicatessens and grocery stores ordered price tickets, window signs and advertisements. He was ignorant of how to do many of the jobs, but a retired missionary from China, Robert Powell, gave him many useful hints along with his future wife's uncle, Mr. Percy Tassell of the Rich Sign Company who introduced him to special paints for signboards and large wall maps and other special jobs he was asked to do. This work enabled Wilf to earn his board money outside of lectures and study periods.

He had gone into the institute feeling the need of the Chinese people for the gospel message and quickly discovered there were many Chinese people in Perth, so it was obvious to him that was where he would start his missionary work. He visited Chinese laundries and fruit shops, then learned about the Chinese Church. It wasn't long before he was teaching in a Chinese Sunday school and even preaching in the church. Chinese Christians took him into their homes and taught him to eat with chopsticks and to write Chinese characters, and he found them to be very generous with both their friendship and gifts.

Over the two years, many missionaries visited the Bible College presenting convincing talks about the desperate need of people without Christ in countries such as Nepal, Russia, South America and Africa. The "three Freds", missionaries to the Kayapo Indians, had just been murdered in Brazil and Wilf wanted to go and take the place of one of the Freds who had come from Belfast. He was torn from one country to another when he heard of their spiritual plight, then unexpectedly two women came from the Badjaling Mission, a small work among Australian Aborigines in the wheatbelt of Western Australia.

Each night he would pray earnestly for God to show him where he could serve and told the Lord he would be willing to go to Russia, Nepal, to the head of the Xingu River in Brazil to replace the murdered Fred, and that he was still willing to go to China. But the voices of the two women from Badjaling kept quietly invading his thoughts. As he prayed he couldn't get rid of the still, small voice that said, "What about the Aborigines?" He tried to push it aside. There were other people at the institute who could answer that call, but his calling was to more romantic locations. "Oh no, Lord!" he prayed. "Anybody can go to the Aborigines, but I am educated now." In his mind he argued that his future was more significant than Aboriginal mission work.

The voice went quiet. For two weeks his prayers seemed to go no higher than the ceiling, then finally he said, "Lord, I'm willing to go to the Aborigines," with the idea in his mind that it would be Arnhem Land or North Queensland. But the voice said, "What about Badjaling?" This was the last straw. From the seeming adventure of going to the heights of Nepal or the depths of the Amazon jungle, the Lord was asking him to go to a place almost a stone's throw from Perth. He was about to argue again, but recalled the agony of two weeks with a heaven of brass above, so surrendered to God's will. The next step was to show his willingness by action, so wrote to Miss Belshaw and Miss McRidge, the elderly missionary partners at Badjaling, and asked if he would be in the way if he came to help them over Christmas. Their reply was a warm welcome.

During his stay at the Bible Institute, Wilf discovered that he now belonged to a very large family. A word from Psalm 68:8 impressed itself on him early in his Christian life: "God setteth the solitary in families." This word would mean a lot more to him later, but at the time he began to realise that the Christian family was scattered worldwide. Apart from the students and staff, who became lifelong friends, there were missionaries from many fields who accepted him as a brother in the Lord. Then, outside the institute, he learned that he had many Chinese brothers and sisters, as well as people from many other nationalities.

One of the jobs he found during his second year was for a Welshman who sold fruit at the Subiaco Open Markets once a week. Wilf discovered that David Gwynne and his wife were keen Christians and during vacations invited him to their orchard at Roleystone on the Darling Range. He was able to earn some extra pocket money here, but also found he was part of a new family. The Gwynnes remained firm friends and supporters over the years.

For his twenty-first birthday, the students gave Wilf a warm overcoat. At the end of 1938, Wilf finished at the college and his fellow students were scattered to many parts of the world as missionaries: to Africa, India, South America, Japan, Papua New Guinea, and many different home ministries.

Beth Weir and Wilf Douglas were both to work with the Aboriginal people of Australia, but in different missions. It was many years before they would meet again. Before Christmas of that year, another student,

Merv Frost took Wilf as a pillion rider on his motorbike to visit his relatives in Bruce Rock then travelled back along the York railway line to Badjaling where he delivered Wilf before continuing on to his home in Wagin.

It was not long before Wilf learned that Miss Belshaw had come to Australia from his own hometown of Belfast, Northern Ireland. Miss McRidge told him that her birthplace was a lighthouse in South Australia. Both women had worked with the Aborigines Inland Mission in New South Wales before they came west to start the children's home at the United Aborigines Mission (UAM), Mt. Margaret Mission. Wilf told the women his story as well, explaining how his father had sent him to Australia from Belfast before he was twelve years of age, and that he had not seen his parents since.

After they became acquainted, preparations had to begin for the Christmas festivities. Wilf's first job was to repair a number of broken toys that had been sent to the mission. Miss Belshaw became occupied in what was called the tin room where she sold secondhand clothes to the women. Miss McRidge attended to the people who came with various physical complaints, such as headaches, colds, cuts, or simply to share their problems or joys.

Uncle Lionel Yarran, Bob Mead, Granny and Jack McKay, the Yarran and Winmar young men, all turned up to help get things ready on Christmas morning. Strings were tied on the clothesline with apples dangling on the ends of them. The big bough shed in the mission yard was re-covered with bushes to supply the shade. The ground was swept ready for the running races and the other sports of the day. Behind the scenes, one of the men was being dressed up as Father Christmas.

It was a wonderful time for Wilf to meet all the people. Families came from Yoting and Shackleton, from Danging and Quairading, from Kellerberrin and York, from wheat farms and from the bush. There was food, fun and gifts for everyone. When all the excitement was over outside, everybody gathered in and around the corrugated iron church to sing hymns, to give testimonies and to listen to the Word of God. The two missionaries encouraged Aboriginal participation in every aspect of the work from involvement in the education of their children to responsibility in the church. The testimonies given by the people were an education and inspiration to Wilf.

When the festivities were over and most people had returned to their homes or work places, Miss Belshaw called Wilf into the mission house living room for a talk. Miss McRidge joined them and both of the women explained to him how tired they had become because there had been no one to relieve them. They asked him if he would be willing to stay for a while and look after the mission while they took a month's holiday. At twenty-one years of age with no other home in Australia, he was glad to accept their request.

It was while he was on his own at Badjaling that Fairbridge sent him his back wages, a total of thirty pounds, equivalent to about two months' wages for a full time factory worker. Getting the money led him to pray about going back to Ireland as he had heard that his mother was very ill. He asked the Lord to show him what to do, and told him that if he didn't want him to go back to Belfast he would rather he took his mother home to himself instead of her having to lie and suffer. The next day, he got a letter from an auntie in Belfast telling him that his mother had died and that his father would be marrying again.

There were very few people in Badjaling at the time. Auntie Jo was camped up near the sandhill, and others like Bob Mead and Billy Garlett, were out hunting. He took his sorrow to the Lord. He felt sure he wasn't to go back to Ireland, so he prayed that if the Lord wanted him to stay at Badjaling he would move the two missionaries to ask him to stay and take over the school.

The day came when Miss Belshaw and Miss McRidge were due back and Wilf went to the Badjaling siding to wait for the train. It was easy to see the diesel electric railcar coming from the Quairading direction. It stirred up a cloud of dust as it sped along the line near the bottom fence of Minchin's farm. Then it slowed down and blew a shrill siren as it came to the cattle pit in the rabbit-proof fence, just before the crossing.

As the single railcar pulled into the siding, Wilf could see Miss Belshaw already standing at the doorway with the suitcases at her feet. As he reached up to take the luggage from the high step, Miss Belshaw said in a broad Belfast dialect, "Och, it's wonderful to have an Irishman meet you at the train. May and I have been talking, and we wondered if you would stay at Badjaling and take over the school!"

Wilf knew straightaway what God wanted him to do. So it was, when school started in February, Miss Belshaw took him over to the corrugated iron building and introduced him to the thirty-eight Badjaling children. She said in her good Irish fashion, "You all know what you don't know, so help Mr. Douglas teach you." Miss Belshaw had already shown him the books she had been using in the school; but there was a lot he had to learn himself, so was thankful that these boys and girls were so patient and well-behaved.

At Fairbridge, Wilf had been well disciplined and learned a lot about physical training and gymnastics, so every morning he started school with a drill parade outside. The children seemed to enjoy the exercises and some of their energy was used up so that they remained quiet in school at least until morning break. Lessons began with Scripture and singing, and then the main emphasis was on the three Rs, interspersed with general knowledge, storytelling, geography and social studies, starting from the known and progressing to the unknown.

9
Joining the Military

A corporal thrust a rake into Wilf's hand and ordered him to rake the ground. The new recruit looked around at the gravel, wondering what needed raking, but enthusiastically set about doing what he had been told.

The Corporal's voice boomed out again, "Hi, mate, not so much hurry. Do you know what an officer looks like? One of those fellows with the pips on his shoulders; when you see one of those fellows coming along, start raking. We've got no other jobs to give you to do, so don't finish too soon!"

War had been raging in Europe and Asia for the two years Wilf had been teaching at the Badjaling school, but it seemed a world away until the day an official letter arrived, addressed to him, requesting that he report for compulsory military training. The children were in tears as they gathered on the railway siding watching the train carrying their beloved teacher away to a distant war. Within days of reporting to the recruitment base at the Claremont Showgrounds he found himself in the Great Southern town of Narrogin where he heard that an appeal had gone out for personnel to apply for the position of signaller for 3rd Field Regiment Artillery. He reported for the position and the next day was assigned to an electricity and magnetism training class where he was introduced to volts, amps, ohms, electrical circuitry, batteries, lamps and Morse code. Within a few weeks he was placed with the Artillery Signallers and worked on line telegraph until assigned to the Observation Post (OP) position with a Lieutenant and another signaller.

The trainees lived in tents at the Narrogin base, taking turns doing guard duty, and running out telephone cables from the OP position to the guns. They would cut cables to pass them under the railway lines, then rejoin them, and after all that, would watch the gunners rip up the cables with shrapnel shells during practice shoots. It proved particularly difficult to join two bare wires when an impatient officer was cranking a distant phone at the same time, and on one occasion Wilf clipped a spare phone on the cable and asked the officer to be patient while the cable was being laid. The officer happened to be the colonel attempting to get through to regimental headquarters, and when he was told there was no link between this cable and the headquarters he demanded that he find one. Fortunately, Wilf was close to a ten-line exchange in a nearby trench, so ran a cable across, bared a wire and joined it to the other system, then calmly informed the colonel, "Through, Sir."

Then the 101 Wireless Transceivers were introduced to the signalling unit and Wilf was sent to a radio school to learn how to use them. The transceivers were used at the Observation Posts ahead of the artillery guns in manoeuvres all over the southwest of Western Australia. As there were fears of a Japanese landing at any place on the West Australian coast, they were kept on the move, opening gates on farms and leading twenty mile-long convoys across paddocks and through scrub and sandhills.

Later the troop was disbanded and all the equipment was handed over to a Special Mobile Force. Wilf found himself at the Northam camp, east of Perth. Here he was placed in charge of a regimental aid post with ten beds and a daily queue of patients needing medical attention.

At first there was a doctor available, and he learned how to treat most cases and how to run the dispensary, then all doctors were called away for field exercises, and Wilf was left to look after the bed patients and the thirty or more soldiers who lined up each day for treatment. Their complaints ranged from hangovers to diarrhea and German measles.

The regimental aid post gave Wilf valuable experience in medicine and in human psychology, however, because he was still a gunner in the artillery, and his regiment was no longer in the area, he received no pay or leave for a considerable time. Eventually, the Australian Army Medical Corps discovered that a non-medical person was operating one of their aid posts and the AAMC major and a sergeant visited the post. Wilf was asked many questions and was given extended leave.

On his return from leave, Wilf was told he was being transferred to a unit that was going to New Guinea. A sergeant accompanied him to Perth and somehow mistook the name of the unit to which he had been assigned, so, instead of going to New Guinea he was sent to Meekatharra, in the Western Australian hinterland, attached to a transport unit as a medical worker. The unit was operating between the railhead at Meekatharra and a secret airfield about 700km north near Marble Bar. Ted Humble, a Christian, and Wilf were the only non-gamblers on the medical team, so when they were not on convoy, they did a bit of gold prospecting, until they discovered the local hospital needed help, so worked there at the Army's expense. While one of them was on convoy duty, the other stayed at the hospital. This gave the men valuable medical experience and they enjoyed sharing their faith with the patients, until Ted, a married man, fell in love with the hospital cook.

When the transporting job was finished, Wilf was transferred to an officers' hospital near Fremantle, then to the camp hospital on Rottnest Island. Spending their time in bed with all windows blacked out at night to prevent lights being seen, the patients were bored, so Wilf determined to find a way to brighten their situation. He began to do crayon drawings on the black-out paper over the windows, then, as he had also done at the Northam RAP, invited men with specialist skills to run classes for the patients in subjects such as art and mathematics, electrical work and motor mechanics.

Wilf's next transfer took him to the Hollywood Military Hospital near Perth where his first appointment was in the casualty ward. On this ward he found conditions as diverse as AIF men who had returned from the Middle East with leg amputations and shell shock, American sailors who had come in for appendix operations; locally based soldiers who were suffering from vehicle and other accidents, and after the bombing of Darwin and Broome, there were many burns victims.

It didn't take long for Wilf to get to know the patients, and to share his faith with them, taking particular interest in men of many different nationalities, including Chinese from labour gangs, Indonesians, Dutchmen and Americans. It was at Hollywood that Wilf began to see a valuable link between his interest in languages, and his artistic abilities. Later in his life he was able to draw on lessons learned at the hospital to illustrate parts of the body in Aboriginal languages. A badly injured Netherlands seaman began teaching Wilf Dutch and eventually he was able to read the Dutch Bible to many other men from Holland and Indonesia. When he began to work in the theatre he watched with interest as top surgeons operated on badly injured soldiers, taking notice of every aspect of their work. He began to assist surgeons and other medical staff by preparing physiological charts, clinical illustrations and diagrams of theatre apparatus, and as a result was given the opportunity to move around with the doctors as they attended clinical meetings and lectures.

After being exposed to many other aspects of life and work in a big military hospital, the Army rediscovered that he was A1 medically and not eligible to be at a home base. Accordingly, again a sergeant took him to a mobilisation centre supposedly to leave for New Guinea in a few days. The major of the new unit called Wilf to his office and remarked that the hospital registrar had indicated that he had been doing artwork for them at the hospital. "The only artwork we would want you to do in this unit would be to paint the word 'man' on a piece of board to nail outside the toilet." He told him that his unit would be leaving for New Guinea in a few days, and recommended he report to the major in the nearby survey unit.

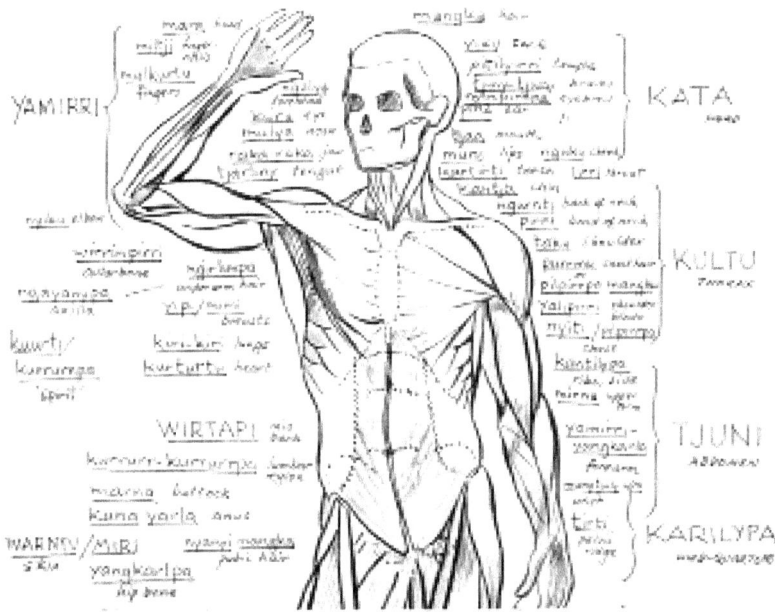

A study of physiology became valuable in later language studies

On reporting to the survey group, Wilf was given a map lettering test and on the following Monday was transferred to the 4th Field Survey Company as a topographical draughtsman. His first job was to make traverses of aerial photographs of the Kimberley region of Western Australia, for the purpose of mapmaking. The knowledge gained from this exercise was of great value later when missionary work took him to Derby and Sunday Island in the Kimberley region.

While he was working at this survey job at the Karrakatta Military Camp, Wilf met Chaplain Robert Haley, previously pastor of the

Maylands Baptist Church who informed him that steps were being taken to have him "manpowered" out of the army to return to teaching in an Aboriginal school. On January 25, 1944, just over two years after enlisting with the 3rd Field Regiment Artillery, Wilf was called into the major's office. Behind him stood a sergeant, and on the other side of the table sat the major and a lieutenant. The major read aloud a statement that he was to be manpowered out of the army immediately unless he belonged to a trade group which made him ineligible for discharge. The major looked up at a chart on the wall and turning to the lieutenant asked, "But Douglas is a TG1 (Trade Group 1) topographical draughtsman, so therefore ineligible for discharge."

The lieutenant, who had been withholding his additional Trade Group pay while he kept the pressure on Wilf to join the permanent force, spluttered something about the trade grouping not having come through yet. The major looked up at the young soldier in front of him and asked, "But you have been receiving your TG1 pay?" Wilf's reply, "No Sir!" was almost drowned out by the lieutenant trying to explain, "There was a reason..." and the major bellowing, "There can be no reason... And now there's no reason why Douglas shouldn't be discharged. He's discharged!" The sergeant behind him asked, "When, Sir?" The major grasped the paper in front of him and read out, "...to be discharged immediately," then he added, "that means now!"

The sergeant drove Wilf to the Claremont camp where he was rushed through the demobilisation procedures and passed through the gates in a daze. His friends, the Winton family, lived nearby, so he visited them and told them the news. Chaplain Haley had told him he would need to apply officially to the United Aborigines Mission. Previously, Wilf had been a voluntary worker only and since Badjaling had been his only home since leaving the Bible Institute, he expected to be reappointed to the school, but on reaching the mission, was told he had been assigned to the Gnowangerup Mission where he would be in charge of a school of forty-three Aboriginal children.

10
Natives in Church

Forty-three little faces looked up at the new schoolteacher. At the front, smiles beamed from the smallest children, but the faces seemed more pensive towards the back of the class where the older children and teenagers sat. Wilf looked around at the class wondering what to expect. He had never been trained as a teacher, in fact he hadn't even been to secondary school, but had developed some skills in the school at Badjaling, and was prepared to do the best he could for this new class of children at Gnowangerup in the far south of Western Australia.

A strict daily routine had already been set out for him, but he had found half an hour the previous evening, all that he was to get each day, to drop into the one-room school and write up some arithmetic sums and problems on the blackboard. He had looked around the classroom and found some old *Beacon* readers and other old books that had been packed in sacks along with secondhand clothing, donations to the mission from the city churches. After his initial introduction to the children, the young school teacher got all the children up to do drill, before getting down to teaching the three Rs: reading, writing and 'rithmetic.

Hedley Wright and his wife, commonly known as Brother and Sister Wright, began missionary work in the Gnowangerup area in 1926. By the time Wilf arrived, the mission station had grown to include a large residence for the Wright family, a trading store, a school building, also used as a church, a dairy which consisted of a simple cowshed, several cows, and a separating room, a fowl run, a bicycle-hiring business, a wool shed for the buying, storing and packing of "dead" wool, and a number of other facilities including a medical post.

Although it was his first day of teaching at the little mission school, Wilf was already tired. The previous day, Sister Wright had showed him to a little two-room cottage where he would sleep at night after a hard day's work. It turned out he wasn't the first single missionary at the mission, and he learned that one by one they had left after discovering the work that was involved. By six a.m. he had already milked the cows, and had fed the calf before breakfast, then went to help Brother Wright serve in the store, selling bread, biscuits, cool drinks and tobacco, until nine o'clock when school started.

When school finished, the day was just underway for the new young missionary fresh out of the army. From four p.m. Sister Wright had organised Wilf to pump up water from an underground tank into the house supply tank, then milk the cows and separate the milk before cleaning up the milk separator. After that, it was into the store with Brother Wright until after dark, usually 7:30 or 8:00 p.m. Sister Wright supplied him with a hot meal every evening, and he was expected to eat this meal with Brother and Sister and their son, Alwyn, who had a club foot.

Immediately after the evening meal, Brother Wright would take Wilf back to the store again to serve the Aboriginal men who had come in from the more distant farms, then they would go to the wool room to weigh the dead wool they had brought in. Dead wool was the wool the men and women had picked off sheep that were found dead in the paddocks of surrounding farms. The men brought the wool into the mission in sugar bags, the hessian bags in which fifty pounds of sugar was sold. In the wool room their task was to run their hands around, inside bags of stinking wool to make sure the weight had not been increased by the addition of bones, stones or other objects. On a Saturday night, they were often in the wool shed until nearly midnight weighing wool, then calculating how much credit each man had for store purchases.

When things were quiet, Wilf would be invited to spend the evening in the Wrights' home making model aeroplanes or playing board games with Alwyn who proved to be a rather demanding child.

Two things impacted Wilf at Gnowangerup. The first was insufficient suitable educational material available to Aboriginal children and Wilf was determined to do something about supplying this need. The other was the level of racial prejudice that existed in this small wheatbelt town. "Natives are not allowed in here!" was a sign that took various forms at the swimming pool, the town hall and at some shops or cafes. Even the churches did not have a welcome for people of Aboriginal descent.

Wilf felt uncomfortable on the day a group of girls from the Gnowangerup mission were to participate in a concert at the Baptist Church in town. Church services were usually held at the mission, but on this occasion, Brother Wright had asked permission of the Baptist Church deacons to allow him to bring a group of Aboriginal girls to sing at a church concert that had been promoted locally. While Wilf wanted to go to the concert with the girls, he had heard about the many objections the deacons had made about the visit. Brother Wright told Wilf how he had met with the deacons and assured them that all the children would be bathed and nicely clothed. The deacons eventually agreed to the idea on certain conditions.

On the day of the concert the children were loaded on to the back of the mission utility truck to make the trip of just over two kilometres into town. Following the conditions set down by the deacons, the truck was driven to the rear of the church. The guests, both church members, and members of the community filed in through the front door of the church, unaware of the group of Aboriginal children who were gathering around the back door. Sitting comfortably in their seats and wearing their best clothes, the congregation enjoyed musical presentations by a number of people, then to the shock of many who held strong opinions about the separation of Aboriginal and non-Aboriginal people, a small group of Aboriginal girls filed in the back door of the church and lined up on the platform. The girls were dressed beautifully and smiled widely as they sang a hymn they had been taught at the mission. When their song was finished they filed silently out the back door, climbed aboard the mission utility and headed back to the mission. As requested by the deacons, they were far away from the main entrance to the church by the time the congregation left the building. Despite all the conditions being carried out faithfully, one of the deacons resigned from the church because the other deacons had allowed "natives" into the church.

Wilf tossed and turned as he lay in bed thinking about the incident, running over in his mind the stark divisions that existed in the community and how they conflicted with his own experiences and beliefs. He also thought about the amount of work that was expected of him and the increasing pressure he was feeling. Brother Wright worked very hard and sometimes Wilf would accompany him when he drove out to pick up a sick person or when he would take some men out to work on a distant farm. As he lay awake he recalled one of those trips when Brother Wright began to teach him a song he had learnt when he had attended a missionary training college in the Eastern States. But as he sang, the vehicle began winding across the road and ran close to a deep drain at the side of the road. Brother Wright had been singing in his sleep and Wilf had to take action to save them from rolling over.

Brother Wright spent much of his time in the store, but he also hired out bicycles, picked up the sick and took them to hospital when necessary, found employment for both men and women, dealt with the buying and selling of dead wool, kept cows and poultry, sold secondhand clothing, and was the undertaker for the Aboriginal people of the area. On one occasion, Wilf worked with Brother Wright until three o'clock in the morning making a coffin for a dead child. He covered the little casket with white cloth and asked Wilf to paint flowers on it while he fixed the chromium plated handles and nameplate in readiness for the burial of the child at six o'clock in the morning.

As he lay there, his mind flashing from one event to another, his thoughts strayed towards Treacy, an attractive young Aboriginal girl who would lean against the corner verandah post looking at him with longing eyes as he served customers at the mission store through an open shutter window. The Aboriginal people were not allowed inside the store but would line up at the window, and in the corner of his eye she was always there. He was desperately lonely and even Treacy's mother had noticed this and had come to him one day.

"Mr. Douglas, you must be very lonely living in that little cottage by yourself. Now, my Treacy is a lovely girl. She has worked in the white fellows' houses and knows how to make beds and everything. Now, she would make a lovely wife for you."

He found Treacy very attractive, but was torn because Sister Wright had warned him many times, "never marry a native girl." He tried to put Treacy out of his mind and tried to recall the words of Scripture he had read the previous morning. He would rise early in the morning each day to read the Bible and pray in order to maintain his spiritual health. His mind wandered to Lois, the Wrights' daughter who was away at teacher training college. On her rare visits home, they had become good friends, but Wilf felt that her mother regarded him as "the worker", a person who could be patronised, but not accepted into the family. Lois and Wilf broke the rules occasionally and enjoyed time together, but the friendship never developed. He thought about a friend of Lois who visited the mission on one occasion, an energetic girl who was clearly attracted to him, but she left disappointed when he made it clear he was looking for a wife who was committed to the Lord and to a missionary call to Aboriginal Australia.

Then he remembered Little Miss Weir, a fellow student at Perth Bible Institute. Beth Weir was born at Brown Hill, near Kalgoorlie, on the 1st of February 1914. Her mother, Mabel Weir (nee Mercer), was a member of a Baptist Church and was a woman of prayer. Many missionaries on the field must have been protected and helped by her faithful remembrance of them daily. Robert Weir, Beth's father, was a godly man with a Methodist background. He had been a printer and bookbinder with the West Australian Government Printing Works.

As a teenager, and prior to going to Perth Bible Institute, Beth had assisted at Badjaling Mission, then after their Bible Institute training, when Wilf went to Badjaling, Beth went to work at Roelands Mission, near Bunbury, on the west coast south of Perth. Now, as Wilf began to pray about his loneliness, he made a decision to write a letter to Beth. School holiday break was coming up and the Wrights' son, Alwyn, was in hospital in Perth for treatment on his club foot. It seemed a safe opportunity to invite Beth to join him in visiting Alwyn in hospital, and afterwards to visit Beth's family home in Bayswater.

It didn't take long for the couple to realise they were meant for each other. But were soon to discover that their lives would not be their own if they were to marry and become missionaries together. They were working for different missions, so each of them had to advise their respective mission headquarters in the Eastern States of their intention to marry. Beth wanted to join the United Aborigines Mission to work with Wilf, so had to ask the UAM Federal Council in Melbourne to consider their proposed marriage. Fortunately, the president of the WA Council, Reverend Edward Hogg, knew both Wilf and Beth, was happy about their union and ultimately conducted their wedding in the Bayswater Baptist Church. The state council was willing to accept them both as missionaries of the UAM "in full standing without the necessity of reapplying", but after they had tied the knot, the Federal Council in Melbourne demanded that they both reapply to the UAM.

Reluctantly, the Wrights accepted the decisions that had been made and that Beth would soon move to Gnowangerup. They knew this would create a change in the relationship they had with Wilf as a young single man who had no other responsibilities than those demanded by the mission. The time he spent assisting Brother Wright would be compromised once he had to consider the needs of a wife. They allocated a small cottage for use by the newlweds and in any free time he could find leading up to the wedding, Wilf tidied up the cottage for Beth, painting it pink and green.

It was a cold night and drizzly rain had set in when the train pulled into Mt. Barker railway station. The young couple had a short honeymoon in Albany and was returning to Gnowangerup where they were to work together as newly-married missionaries. They expected Brother Wright to drive in from Gnowangerup to pick them up, but as they sat in the cold, it slowly occurred to them he wasn't coming, and they would have to spend the night in the railway station to catch the next train to Gnowangerup the following morning. Next to the railway station was a dilapidated railway shed with a large hole in the middle of the floor. There was an old spring mattress over the hole and the couple spread their coats over the mattress in an effort to make a bed. They tried to lie down for a while, but the cold wind blew through the hole and the rusty springs squeaked, so they spent much of the night walking up and down the railway line in an attempt to keep warm.

Home for the newly-weds in Gnownangerup

Local Christians from the town and nearby farms were encouraged by the Wrights' to give them a tin-kettling on their first night in the cottage, but difficulties developed quickly, as Wilf was no longer a single worker at the beck and call of the missionaries-in-charge. Instead of spending every free night playing with Alwyn, Wilf wanted to go home to his wife and when he had finished in the store, he was eager to go home for a hot drink instead of accompanying Brother Wright to his house. The relationship between the newly married missionary couple and the Wrights was beginning to sour.

As workers in the United Aborigines Mission, missionaries were expected to rely on God alone for the supply of their needs and any donations of money to the mission were equally divided between all the missionaries, apart from specific donations to missionaries from their home church or interested friends. Beth had transferred from another mission to the UAM at the time of their marriage and Wilf had had no real church connections before he became a missionary, so their income averaged about five pounds per month, essentially enough for food to last a few weeks.

One day, they had only sixpence left and Brother Wright was going into town to do the shopping. He asked them if they needed anything, so they ordered sixpence-worth of soup bones. When he got back he had brought four shillings-worth of meat saying that he thought sixpence-worth of soup bones would not go very far. The situation became very embarrassing when they refused to accept the meat, unwilling to tell the Wrights they couldn't afford the purchase.

Beth helped Wilf in the school by taking the infant class, and they were very happy working together, but the heavy work and the strain of their relationship with the founding missionaries eventually took their toll on Wilf's health. Catching the flu, he went downhill very rapidly, and it was suggested they go to Perth for a week's holiday. While there, the state council of the mission met with them and asked them both to go to Badjaling, which was now without a missionary presence.

They had both lived at Badjaling previously, so they were very excited to arrive at their old home, now as a married couple, but most of the locals had gone away after Christmas and Wilf and Beth found themselves alone and very short of food. They wondered if their circumstances were caused by them not doing enough missionary work to warrant financial support from interested Christians in the city, so Wilf walked into Quairading to give out Christian tracts to the white residents, somehow easing his conscience that he was being faithful in the service to God.

Walking back from Quairading one day, Wilf met Billy Garlett coming along the road with a turnout almost full of skinned rabbits. Wilf asked him what he was going to do with them, and he told him he was selling the skins and just throwing the rabbits out in the bush.

Billy said, "You can have one if you want it Mr. Douglas."

Wilf picked up one rabbit and ran home to Beth who cooked it for tea. Apart from the rabbit, they only had some Weetbix in the house. However, shortly afterwards, another local man came back from Quairading where he had been selling his vegetables. He walked into the kitchen and shook out one of his wheat bags and out fell a cabbage and some other vegetables he hadn't sold. He was expecting to have tea with them, so Beth told Wilf to keep him occupied by playing draughts until she had cooked the rabbit and the vegetables. The situation wasn't so simple when someone brought in a side of sheep and offered it to them for four shillings. They had no money so had to refuse it, once again, too embarrassed to say they couldn't afford the meat.

While they were battling their own issues, Wilf and Beth had other matters to address. An epidemic of gastro enteritis swept through the Aboriginal population and in one week alone, Wilf was asked to take seven funerals for Badjaling babies. Day after day he would drive the undertaker's hearse, an old T Model Ford with only two gears working, to the Quairading cemetery. As he threw the vehicle into top gear it jerked forward as Wilf watched buggies and turnouts that were heading to the funeral, run off the road to avoid bumping into him, often getting bogged in the sand in the process.

The gravity of the situation was only lightened as Wilf recalled the story he had been told about the time the whole camp thought their babies had been stolen during a gambling game. Algie Kickett had come home from his farm job with an unusually big pay cheque. Gambling was a popular activity and they say that Algie lost his horse and buggy in the game that went on through the night. As they played, the excitement of the game mounted and mothers forgot about their babies. Mona Kickett was only a girl herself, but she was unable to sleep, listening to the sound of babies crying in the camps while hearing the excited voices from the camp where the game was being played. Mona got up quietly and moved around the camps where she could hear the crying. She picked up each of the babies and took them back to her camp and put them to bed.

At about two o'clock in the morning, a cry went out: "My baby's gone." Alarmed at the news the other the mothers rushed to their camps only to find their babies were also missing. A great wailing spread through the bush as people began to inquire what had happened. Christianity had a strong influence in the small Badjaling community, so the guilt associated with the gambling, as well as traditional superstitions combined with fear to led to the assumption that God had taken their babies away in punishment for their gambling. Finally, someone discovered the babies in Mona's camp, but as the mothers rushed to recover their babies they were met by Mona who stopped them at the entrance to her camp: "Don't touch the babies," she told the panic-stricken mothers. "Jesus has tucked all your babies up in bed. So they have to stay here for the rest of the night."

11
Kimberley Bound

Dark clouds gathered on the horizon as the State Ship *MV Koolinda* headed out from Fremantle Harbour. As night fell, the wind picked up, and the 100 metre long steel-hulled ship became the victim of high winds and heavy seas. The storm intensified as the night progressed and passengers found themselves being violently flung around their cabins. The ship was to travel north along the West Australian coast with live sheep, perishable goods to be offloaded at the various ports along the coast, eventually stopping at Darwin where a large group of women who had been evacuated during the war were heading to re-establish their homes.

The crew had been on strike the previous day and some valves had not been tightened so water entered the engine room and the holds. Then the pumps broke down and the ship got a heavy list to the starboard so that it became impossible to turn northwards along the coast for fear the ship would roll over. For two days they struggled westward with waves breaking over the decks and running down the companionways. Sheep in the holds were drowned and the crew threw them overboard as they died. Glasses, crockery and cutlery were thrown off the tables in the dining room and scattered across the floor.

Among the passengers were Wilf and Beth Douglas and their nine month old son John, on their way to a new appointment as missionaries with the United Aborigines Mission in Derby, a tiny town at the head of the King Sound in the far north of Western Australia. Overcome by the heat and smell of oil in their cabin, Beth struggled up the steps with her baby holding anxiously to the baby in one hand, while trying to keep her balance by holding on to the handrails on the staircase. They had previously tied their pram to the top of the stairway, but as Beth reached it and bent down to place John into the pram, the ship hit another massive wave and she lost her balance. The baby was thrown out of her arms and down the stairwell. Desperately, Beth made her way back down the stairs to find the tiny baby still wrapped in a blanket and unharmed. She discovered later a stewardess suffered a fractured skull when she hit a bulkhead during the storm. In the meantime, Wilf was unaware of the drama that was unfolding as he was so seasick he remained on his bunk.

When he felt well enough to get up he was able to speak with an engineer whom he discovered was a Christian. This man had worked through all the violence of the storm to keep the engines running and disassembled the pumps ready to put new parts in when the boat reached port. Four days after leaving Fremantle, they returned to port. Tonnes of wet chaff and other goods were lifted out of the holds and dropped into railway trucks to be dumped.

***

Artist, Percy Ivor Hunt was born in Fremantle in 1903, and became well known for his figurative watercolours. He studied in Perth, London and Paris, and spent three years working as a commercial artist in Singapore before returning to Perth in 1938 to teach at Perth Technical College. It was a great surprise to Wilf when he enrolled in a commercial art course at the college to discover he would be studying under this prolific artist. Hunt believed that good drawing was the first essential in commercial art and assigned all sorts of objects to draw in pencil before they were introduced to pen and ink work.

"You must draw the objects until it seems possible to pick the objects off your drawing pad!" he urged. The class graduated from drawing gramophones, cameras, towels, skulls, hats and coats, to drawing classical statues, death masks, then live models.

The twelve month course, included outdoor sketching, pen and ink drawing, watercolours, drapery, ancient and modern design, commercial lettering, fashion drawing, and the preparation of art work for display or for commercial printing. It wasn't long before Wilf realised that God was preparing him for his later work in translation and literacy work for Aborigines.

As 1945 came to an end, the health issues Wilf had experienced at the end of their time in Gnowangerup, were impacting on their ministry at Badjaling, and Beth was pregnant and suffering from asthma, so it became evident a change was necessary. When an opportunity came to undertake a twelve-month commercial art course under a soldiers' rehabilitation scheme, Wilf and Beth moved to Perth at the beginning of 1946. Their first son, John Craig was born in March.

Gnowangerup School had convinced the pair that Aboriginal children needed books that were more applicable to their lives and backgrounds so Wilf was keen to develop his drawing skills to help him achieve this purpose. When applying for the rehabilitation course, he was told that the only category he could fit into was for a course in drawing, which was available for soldiers who had been kindergarten teachers before enlistment. The authorities argued that since Wilf was a teacher of Aboriginal children and Aborigines who "are still in the kindergarten stage", he was eligible to take the course in drawing.

At the end of the year, the mission assigned Wilf and Beth to Derby in the Kimberley region of WA. Despite the small allowance they received while Wilf was a student, by Christmas time they had very little money to start out on a new venture. The mission provided the money to pay their boat fare to Derby, but, when they reached the

State Shipping Office, they learned the fare had increased, and they had to pay the additional amount out of their own savings.

When they reached the Fremantle wharf, they were informed that the crew of the *Koolinda* had gone on strike. They had looked forward to having their evening meal on the ship, but were told no passengers could board the ship until after meal time. They wandered the Fremantle streets with no money in their pockets until they came to the home of a woman who was a friend of Misses Belshaw and McRidge of Badjaling. When she saw them, she said, "Oh dearies, I've been wondering where you two were. I have something in the jar on the mantle shelf for you." She handed them a one-pound note and gave them a meal.

Ship at Derby jetty low tide

Following their disastrous four days at sea they were able to use some of their one pound to pay their fare to Bayswater to visit Beth's mother and stay the night. Next day, they sailed again on the *Koolinda* and had a more restful trip up the West Australian coast.

As most of the perishable cargo had been jettisoned after the storm, crates of beer were about the only items unloaded at each of the ports, much to the dismay of the women who were waiting for their wet-season food supplies. Because of the delay caused by the storm, the tides were not right for the ship to land at Derby, so it carried them on to Wyndham and Darwin.

It was the hottest part of the wet season and the humidity was high. John contracted prickly heat then impetigo and they had to take him to the hospital in Darwin. On the return trip, the purser paid Wilf two pounds for helping unload steel rods at the Wyndham jetty. This and the change from the one-pound had to suffice them for their first two months in Derby. John had to be hospitalised in Derby because his whole skin broke down with impetigo. His life was saved when penicillin was flown up from Perth. They received a bill afterwards for two pounds from the Health Department in Perth.

It was not long before they discovered there were three social classes in Derby, and they were on the lowest level because they associated with the full-blood Aborigines. The mixed-blood people, Malaysian, Chinese, Japanese and Aboriginal, were the middle class and they ran businesses such as the bakery, the butcher and the greengrocer. The upper class was the European Australians who were in shipping, airlines, banking, and the post office. The Aboriginal people from the missions, such as the Presbyterian Mission at Kunmunya, would laugh at the way they were despised by the members of the two other classes.

Wilf and Beth had been sent to Derby to keep the mission work open to the local Aboriginal people while missionary Ern Faulkner and his wife led the work at the inland Mount Barnett settlement. They had arrived at Derby in January at a time when anyone involved in missionary work was aware that donations were scarce. Weeks went by and no money came from the mission council or even a note to ask if they had arrived safely or what work they were doing. Missionaries were expected to operate under the "faith principle" believing that God would meet their needs, but as time went on they began to wonder if there was something wrong with this principle.

They were determined not to go into debt, so Wilf began to work with a local storekeeper he knew in an effort to obtain sufficient funds to feed themselves. However, even as he worked, he battled with his conscience because it seemed to go against the principles of the mission he had committed himself to serve. Conflicted in many ways, Wilf wrote out his resignation and walked to the post office where he posted the letter. Later that day, the mail arrived and in it was a delayed Christmas gift of two pounds. On the one hand, they felt this was a confirmation of their decision to resign, but on the other hand wondered if they had been too hasty.

Unexpected events overruled their decision and they found themselves in the UAM for many more years.

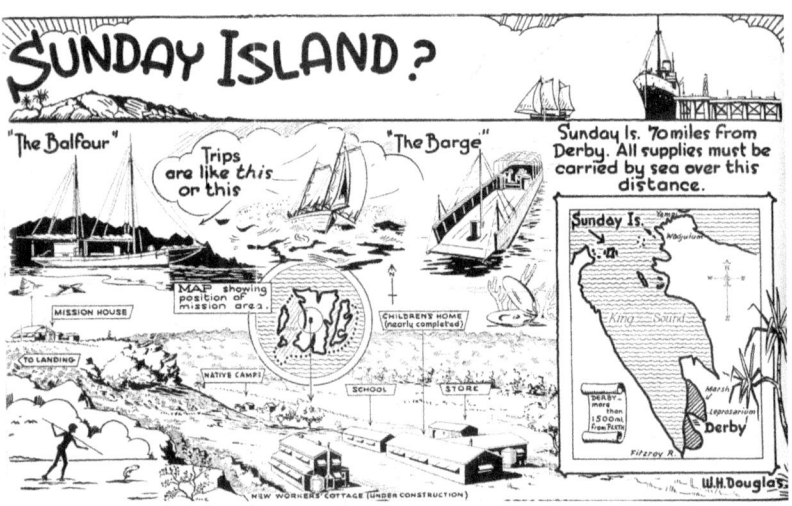

A graphic Wilf drew to describe Sunday Island

12
Sunday Island

The humidity soaked into the night air like a sponge. Even lying perfectly still in bed their skin was damp from perspiration. The twinkling stars provided the only light and in the distance they could hear the roar of the sea as the tidewaters poured off the coral reef that surrounded Sunday Island. It was their first night at the island and Wilf and Beth were lying in separate cyclone wire beds reflecting on the day. They were glad that John had settled down quickly and was sleeping soundly. A cot was the only piece of furniture they possessed and they had brought it with them to the island and set it up in the sleep-out bedroom where the two beds had been placed for their use. Beth had spread a large mosquito net over the cot after they had tucked John in to bed. They made up their beds in the light of a single hurricane lantern, and gladly dropped their tired bodies on to the top of the blankets and blew out the lantern. They lay awake until all was quiet outside except the distant pounding of waves on the reef.

Then they heard another noise. It was like a vibration that was growing louder and louder. As they listened they sensed that it was in the house, and in a vague way the vibration seemed to be in the kitchen. Wilf jumped out of bed and switched on a torch and walked carefully to the kitchen. At first, he could see nothing unusual, then a movement on the walls caused him to shine the torch upwards. The source of the vibration was apparent. The whitewashed walls were black with enormous cockroaches with vibrating wings. He called Beth and they stood amazed at the sight. There was nothing they could do about the problem that night so they went back to the sleepout, made sure John's cot was securely covered, got into bed and closed their ears and thoughts to the black owners of the house.

Later, they were to move into a larger house built of cypress pine and clad with corrugated iron. It was a two-storey house, intended to give the occupiers a view of the sea from the top floor, but the rocky sides of the valley rose two or three more metres above the roof level, so only the superintendent, who lived on top of the hill, had the sea views. With flour and grain stored in one half of the downstairs part of the house, they acquired vermin of a different variety in the new house—rats. They weren't concerned while the rats stayed downstairs, it was when they began to appear in the bedroom upstairs that they decided drastic action was needed to reduce their population. A forty-four gallon drum of water with a baited wire at the top caught a few of the beasts, but Beth brought some peaceful nights to their home in the valley when she organized a children's hunting expedition with the promise of a reward for each rat killed.

The United Aborigines Mission had four workers on Sunday Island at the time the Douglas's arrived in Derby: Mr. Norman Williams was the superintendent; Mr. and Mrs. Preston Walker were in charge of the school and the children's home; Miss Ruth Allen also assisted in the school and the children's home. Just as Wilf and Beth were preparing for the return of the Faulkners to Derby, Mr. and Mrs. Walker resigned from Sunday Island leaving Norman Williams, whose wife was in England at the time, alone with Miss Allen, so Beth and Wilf volunteered to go to Sunday Island for a short time to relieve the situation. Telegrams to Sunday Island had to pass through the local post office, then they would be telegraphed to Wyndham from where they were radioed to the island on the Flying Doctor pedal radio system. Wilf and Beth's offer was accepted by telegram from Mr. Williams.

They sailed to the island on the *Balfour Matthews*, the mission's only lugger and on arrival at the mission landing on the west side of Sunday Island, Norman Williams greeted them with the words, "You two are in charge of the medical work, the children's home and the school teaching." He gave them a house in the deep valley midway between the two major sections of the Aboriginal community. The house was made of corrugated iron, and it had been freshly whitewashed.

***

The school gave them their first conflict with a fellow-worker. Because the superintendent had told Wilf he was in charge of the school, he appeared at the first assembly only to be met by the middle-aged Miss Allen who informed them she was in charge of the school and that, under her supervision, Wilf could take one of the classes. Once they had sorted out the fact that Mr. Preston Walker, the previous headmaster, had appointed Miss Allen to the position and that the mission superintendent had appointed Wilf, the two managed to run the school between them.

The medical work proved to be a daily responsibility. Because Wilf had been a medical worker in the Army, he was concerned about the lack of facilities for treating the various types of injuries and disorders the people suffered, so wrote to the mission secretary in Perth and ordered medicines and equipment which he felt were essential. Because fishing on the coral reef was a regular method for bringing in the daily meat supply of the camp, wounds caused by sharp coral, nail and swordfish, stingrays and clam shells were common, as were sore eyes, burns, stomach upsets, colds and flu. Wounds from fighting called for treatment from time to time.

Their first medical shock, however, was the discovery that all those in the children's home had scabies. Searching the meagre medical kit, there appeared to be nothing that could treat scabies. Then Wilf discovered a large tin of sulphur powder on a top shelf. The men had caught a dugong, so he asked them for some dugong oil, mixed the sulphur into an ointment with the oil, then spread it over the bodies of the children. They closed the school until every trace of scabies had disappeared, which meant that the boys had to move camp so they were not sleeping on the dirt floor of the school at night.

Not long after their arrival on the island, the other missionaries left and Wilf and Beth found themselves alone as the only non-Aboriginal people. Wilf had grown up in the institutional setting at Fairbridge, so as he looked at the health issues faced by the children; he knew that action had to be taken. They were hundreds of kilometres from the mission headquarters so consultation was out of the question. They had to make the decision themselves. Without delay Wilf and Beth took the step to close the children's dormitories and send all the children to their parents who were living in the valley close to the mission. In a short time a change occurred. The children went swimming in the sea every day. They were happier and healthier, caught fish for their families and the scabies and other "dormitory" illnesses disappeared.

***

After the war, Norman Williams had acquired an American landing barge from Champagny Island, where US forces were situated during World War II. The barge was used to help the Sunday Island men collect trochus shell, an activity that helped to boost the economy of the island. The barge had two big Ford V8 marine engines below deck, and it was Wilf's task to keep these engines going when he accompanied the men on trochus shell expeditions to Brue Reef. Sometimes they used the barge to take children for trips to other islands, but it was mainly used for commercial purposes. The lugger also was used for shelling trips. It had a small four-stroke marine engine. When Wilf went with the men to Derby for stores or went on long shelling trips, such as to the Lacepede Islands, it fell to his lot to look after this engine.

The oil filter had the habit of dropping off inside the engine from time to time, and he would regularly stop the engine, remove the sump cover, fish around in the hot oil and find the filter and force it on to the pipe situated between the big ends. When the sea was rough it was a struggle to keep anything in his stomach while he knelt on a board over the swilling and oily bilge water, with a hot exhaust pipe over his head and cockroaches running around the timbers. Many times he had to climb on to the deck to lean over the side, but when he looked into a yawning whirlpool, quickly returned to the engine with the skipper's words ringing in his ears, "Hurry up, Mr. Douglas, we're getting close to those rocks!"

The men expected Wilf to look after the engines, but he left the navigation in the hands of the Bardi men. They were sea people who knew the tides and currents in these wild waters of the Buccaneer Archipelago. Their traditional catamaran rafts were made of two separately bound sets of mangrove trunks placed one on the other. A man would sit where the two parts of the raft overlapped and, with the minimum of paddling, would follow the various currents to the areas in which he intended to fish, collect trochus shell or gather firewood. Only when he needed to cross from one current to another did he paddle more vigorously.

On Wilf's first trip to Brue Reef on the barge he was amazed how far they travelled on the open sea, the Indian Ocean, before the men asked him to stop the engines while they lowered the anchors. There was no land in sight in any direction, and he could see no signs to indicate why the men had decided to anchor in this spot. They ate, then talked and rested for a few hours, then he noticed that the barge was being lowered on to a sand bank. The water had gone down about six metres. Within a short time, they were sitting on a circle of sand in the middle of an enormous coral reef that extended for probably a kilometre in every direction.

As the tide receded, the men would take sacks and walk out on the reef. They appointed Wilf to keep the dinghy afloat in the receding waters so that they would have the boat to carry back their loads of trochus shell. Before they left, Bill Ahchee handed Wilf a spear and said, "If you see one of those big things coming towards your feet, stick this spear into it!" Near the edge of the reef and as the tide returned, the dinghy was loaded with bags of shell. They towed it back through deepening waters until they reached the barge again.

Trochus shells had been collected on the reefs of the Bonaparte and Bucaneer Archipeligo's by the local Aboriginal people for many years and brought a good price as they were used in the production of mother of pearl buttons and various types of jewelry. Rather than dealing directly with possibly unscrupulous dealers, the hunters would return all their shells to the Sunday Island store so that the mission could negotiate sales on their behalf. A record was kept at the store for each of the families and they would draw on the credit they had established whenever they shopped at the mission store. It fell to Wilf, after each trip, to weigh the shell and write down the credit for each family in the store book.

When Harry and Ethel Lupton arrived to take over as superintendent of the mission, Harry led the men in cutting a channel through the mangrove swamp right into the middle of the mission area. The channel was deep enough to allow the barge to approach almost to the store building, thus saving the men the difficult task of carting the shell on their shoulders over the hill from the regular mission landing. This landing was on the west side of the island and it was here that the *Balfour* and the barge were usually anchored.

Soon after the Luptons arrival, they were called away by the UAM council in Perth to go on a secret mission. It was months before they learned that the secret mission was a prospecting trip to Warburton Ranges to investigate a mica deposit. Harry assured them he would not be away for long, so they held the boats in readiness to pick him and his wife up at Derby and refrain from going on shelling trips until after he returned.

It was during Harry's absence that they were struck by the worst cyclone yet experienced. They battened down the shutters on the mission buildings and prepared basins and buckets to catch the water that came through the roof where the pedal wireless pole passed through the corrugated iron above the living room.

At the height of the cyclone, some men pounded on the door to inform Wilf that the barge and the lugger had broken their moorings. He accompanied them over the hill and saw the two vessels drifting out towards the central channel that poured past the island on the west. In the dinghy, they managed to reach the lugger through the howling wind and rain then tried to reach the barge in the lugger. Smashing up against the barge, the timber on the lugger was damaged, but they clambered aboard and Wilf struggled to uncover the engines to try and stop the barge from hurtling through the rushing current towards the south of the island. As the engines spluttered to life and they threw the propellers into reverse, the barge spun around in wild circles grazing against rocks and coral as they attempted to steer it into the new mangrove channel.

As they approached the entrance to the channel at a frightening speed, the chains of the tiller broke and the men lost control of the steering. Rushing to the rear of the barge, Wilf yelled above the noise of wind and sea for three or four men to grasp the steel arm of the tiller and try to steer them toward the channel. This was a Herculean task as the chain and pulley system, which had broken, normally gave a lot more leverage to the tiller. It took all their strength, coupled with fear, for the men to steer with this lack of leverage. They were praying out loud as the barge plunged from the fast current into the quietness of the mangrove channel and lifted their hearts in praise as they realised they were in a safe haven.

***

There were happy times at Sunday Island when, as a family, they walked to the north of the island and played on the beach and swam at Running Waters. The waters here were turquoise in colour and made a picturesque setting for the white sand bay with the view of East and West Roe Islands on the horizon. Other landing places were at Learing Point and at Cocky's Camp. From the superintendent's house on the top of the hill, there was a beautiful view of the coral reef between Sunday Island and its neighbouring Allora Island. To the north, Learing Point could be seen and, beyond, the open sea and the channel between the island and the Roe Islands. It was along this channel the State Steamship *Koolinda* or the *Dorrigo* could be seen as they sailed past on their way to Derby.

On one occasion they saw a whale at the edge of the coral at the north end of the island. It was when the tide drained off the coral that the Bardi people would swarm over the area with their spears to spear the fish caught in the many holes in the reef. Although Wilf and Beth's income came from donations from Christians far from the island and would sometimes drop to a very low level, they were able to trade flower, tea and sugar for fish. The garden also produced mangoes, pawpaws and bananas during the wet season, and also some vegetables. For nine months of the year there was little rain, but during the monsoon period there could be up to 800mm of rain in twenty-four hours.

As missionaries, of course, Wilf and Beth's concern was for the spiritual state of the inhabitants of the island. The Bardi people had been in the habit of attending church ever since the turn of the century when the explorer and pioneer, Sydney Hadley, took a Church of England minister there to confirm and baptise the people. Hadley had established the mission on the island home of the Jawi and Bardi people in 1899, and it was taken over by the United Aborigines Mission in 1923. There were stories that in Hadley's time, the people would acknowledge the symbols of the body and blood of Jesus at the church in the morning, then, in the afternoon, would gather on the other side of the island for a traditional blood-drinking ritual.

Times for church services were governed by the moon and the tides, for when the tides were right, the people had to go fishing for their daily food. There were no refrigerators on the island, so meat had to be caught fresh from the sea when it was available. Once the stomach was satisfied, then people came to the mission church. The men sat at the front and women at the back in respect for the Bardi rule of mother-in-law avoidance and other taboos.

***

Soon after their arrival in the Kimberley before moving from Derby to Sunday Island, Wilf had an experience that set the scene for future language work and the translation of the Bible into Aboriginal languages. He was given the opportunity to join Ron Ross, the superintendent of the Presbyterian mission at Kunmunya to sail from Derby to Kunmunya on board the mission's lugger, the *Watt Leggatt*. The crew was composed of about eight men, mainly from the Worora tribe. Sam, the skipper, was born on Sunday Island. Jimmy, the second in command, came from the Montgomery Islands, and Alan, the engineer was a lad from Kunmunya, who thoroughly understood the twin cylinder diesel engine in the lugger.

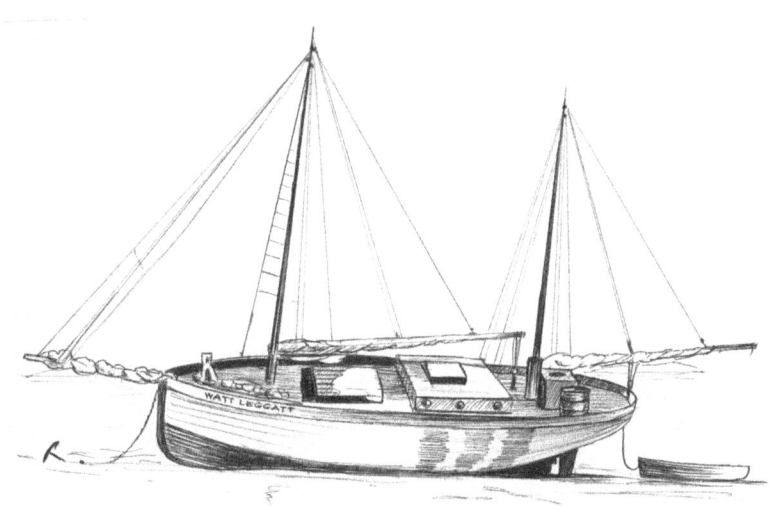

With the approach of darkness came a strong headwind and rough seas. Sam found it necessary to tack at an oblique angle into the wind. It was exhilarating for Ron and Wilf to stand on deck and feel the salt sea spray on their faces, and to watch the white waves dash over the bows, but seasickness spoilt the beauty of the view. They had nothing to eat all day, so retching was dry and hurtful. They tried lying on the roof of the cabin by clinging to the skylight, but the movement became increasingly difficult. At one stage, Wilf tried to make his way to the entrance of the cabin, but a swinging rope from the boom whipped his diary and sketches from his hand and flung them into the raging sea where they disappeared into the darkness.

A bright morning after a stormy night found them anchored by a great rock east of Sunday Island. At sunrise, they moved off again and, after negotiating the island's treacherous waters for over two hours they arrived at a dinghy landing point. Because of the low tide, they could not reach the mission landing on the other side of the island, so had a long walk of two or three kilometres up a rocky hill, down into a muddy inlet, through a mangrove swamp, around a precipitous path, along a winding creek, with heat, grass seeds, flies, and more noticeable, empty stomachs.

It was on this trip that Ron Ross introduced Wilf to the work that was being done with the Worora people at Kunmunya Presbyterian Mission, and in particular the language study that was carried out by J. R. B. Love who had been a schoolteacher there in 1914. It was the result of Love's initiative that the mission was moved from Port George IV to Kunmunya. When he returned to Kunmunya in 1927, he began serious language study and Bible translation. It was this work that was later to become an inspiration to Wilf when he became convinced that language and translation work should be continued among the Aboriginal people of Australia.

Sometime after this trip, Jimmy, the assistant skipper, came to Wilf with a big Authorised Version of the Bible in his hand and asked him if there was something that would help to make the words clear to him. He said he had been reading and reading a verse and could not work out what it meant. In the conversation which followed, Jimmy said, "Oh it would be wonderful, Mr. Douglas, if we had the Bible in Bardi."

On the spot Wilf and Jimmy attempted to write down a translation of John's Gospel chapter three, verse sixteen in Bardi. Wilf wrote down the words, *Lian inamang kalalang purdja amborin*, supposedly meaning, God so loved the world. As he listened to the last word, he realised Jimmy was pronouncing the *n* with his tongue between his teeth, and began to realise that he was not adequately equipped to translate the Bible into Bardi. He didn't know any phonetic symbol for what he was to discover later was an interdental nasal sound, and it began to dawn on him that he was placing quite a burden on Jimmy to find words in Bardi for God, love, and the world.

On board the *Watt Leggatt*

Little did he realise that Wilf's discovery that day represented a change in the way Christian missionaries in Australia began approaching their work. An interest in the language of the Aboriginal people was to see a change of focus towards not only recording people's language, but teaching language and promoting indigenous literacy. For Wilf, it was the start of a journey that would take him far away from the islands in the north of the state, to the red desert at the heart of the continent.

13
Journey to the Desert

Spinifex bushes covered the red sandhills, their sharp spikes pointing upwards to the cloudless sky. Winter in the Western Australian desert is bitterly cold at night, but in the daytime the sun beats down mercilessly, a few gnarled mulga trees that dot the harsh landscape offering the only protection. The track was little more than two rugged wheel ruts in the sand, and the old AEC truck with the rear axle dangling in the dirt painted a forlorn picture.

Six men, three of them Aboriginal and a woman in her thirties were sitting in the dirt on the side of the track, pressing close to the truck to take advantage of the little shade that was offered, and to protect them from the cold morning wind. A seven-year-old boy who seemed to be taking responsibility for the group, stood in front of them, reading from a notebook perched on a wooden fruit case. He called the group to attention, and invited them to sing the National Anthem. Their clothes were dusty and bedraggled, and they looked tired, their voices barely loud enough to sing the words, "God save our gracious Queen". A small Australian flag was fluttering from the truck aerial, as the group of adults bowed their heads reverently while the boy led them in a prayer he read from his notebook.

He Speaks Our Language

The date was June 2, 1953, and as Her Majesty Queen Elizabeth II experienced the pomp and ceremony of her Coronation in England, far away in the Western Australian desert, a seven-year-old boy led an untidy band through what may have been the most isolated coronation service anywhere in the Commonwealth.

For two weeks Wilf and Beth Douglas, their son John, two missionaries with the United Aborigines Mission, and three young Aboriginal men, eked out an existence on the side of the dusty track, their only link to the outside world, a scheduled link-up once a day on an ancient pedal wireless. The rear wheel bearings of the ten tonne truck had collapsed and the heat generated from the collapse had led to the rear axle snapping in half, leaving them stuck hundreds of kilometres from any habitation, a small Aboriginal mission.

Each day, a couple members of the group would walk many kilometres through the bush trying to identify possible water holes where they could salvage enough water in a bucket to bring home to the rest. Water couldn't be wasted on washing or cleaning teeth as every precious drop was needed to keep them alive until a mission representative could make their way to their broken down truck with the necessary parts.

But the time was not wasted. Wilf and Beth noticed that the three young Aboriginal men with them were too frightened to walk to the next waterhole because of the spirit of a dead man who was buried there. Wilf learned that the man's reburial had not been performed, and began to store away in his mind and his notebooks, the new cultural issues he was about to face. He went walking with the Aboriginal men each day, asking questions that would help him to grasp their language. He learned that a skin group system operated at Warburton, and with the help of the men, discovered what his and Beth's skin group was, thus helping them to understand their relationship to everyone in the Western Desert area. This gave them an immediate sense of belonging when they arrived at their new home.

Less than a fortnight before their departure, Wilf and Beth had received a telegram advising them they had been appointed to work as missionaries at Warburton Ranges Mission, situated just south of the Gibson Desert, 1500km east northeast of Perth and 1000km southwest of the central Australian town of Alice Springs. Now on their way to their appointment they found themselves sleeping at night in freezing desert temperatures under the stars, and by day seeking protection from the blazing desert sun.

The young boy who had been inspired by the idea of a coronation ceremony, may have overlooked the desperate nature of their situation, but had an important part to play in maintaining the morale of the adults in the group.

The desert was no stranger to John or to his parents who were following what they believed was God's call to serve the indigenous inhabitants of Australia, and in particular, to understand the language and culture of people they had grown to love. The invitation to Warburton Ranges followed their sudden departure from the isolated sandhills of Ooldea, a tiny railway siding in South Australia, the location of a children's home run by the United Aborigines Mission.

When they left Sunday Island, Beth and John stayed in Perth while Wilf went to Melbourne from January to March 1950, to attend what was called the Wycliffe School of Linguistics for Missionaries, later to become known as the Wycliffe Bible Translators Summer Institute of Linguistics (WBT/SIL). Renowned American linguist, Dr. Ken Pike was the principal of the school and opened Wilf's mind to the world of academia as well as the science of linguistics. The SIL course challenged Wilf's thinking in a way he had never experienced. Each day Ken Pike gave his students grueling drills in an effort to get them to use parts of their brains that had been lying dormant. Convinced that Wilf had the capacity to go further, he challenged him daily, sitting him down on his bedroom floor with a chart and drilling him in the use of "glided and unglided vocoids", which Wilf was to discover included addressing his Irish accent and the way he pronounced "oo" sounds.

Their time on Sunday Island helped Wilf and Beth to crystallise their thinking about many aspects of missionary work. They experienced Christian fellowship with local Aboriginal couples, and saw themselves as fellow Christians with them rather than missionaries who were there to impose Christianity on the "natives." They were angered by many of the decisions made in Melbourne by well-meaning mission directors then and in years to come. Conversations with missionaries at the SIL school who were working with different missions all over the world came as a breath of fresh air.

Since their time at the Gnowangerup Mission School Wilf had carried the burden of providing written literature that was more suitable for people who did not have a written language. His rehab course in commercial art gave him a tool to experiment in presenting the gospel message in a picture form that would be understood by non-readers. After Wilf had drawn "The Two Ways", he used his deferred army pay to produce a five-colour lithographed poster that was eventually translated into many languages around the world and was used for many years as a standard gospel tool.

Wilf and Beth's decision to investigate how linguistics could help them engage better with Aboriginal people and enable them to read the Bible in the language they understood best attracted opposition from the least expected source. During their time at the SIL school they had assumed they would be returning to Sunday Island to carry out Bible translation, but were devastated when they received a letter from mission headquarters telling them they could not return to the Kimberley as their interest in language work would lead Aboriginal people back into heathenism. The news left them confused and bewildered, so when an opportunity arose for Wilf to attend a year-long course in linguistics at Sydney University it appeared a new door was opening. The course was due to start immediately after the SIL school in Melbourne concluded.

The year of study at Sydney University resulted in Wilf being awarded a diploma of anthropology, and it was an opportunity for him to stretch his mind even further. The mission invited Wilf and Beth to work with the Aboriginal church at La Perouse during their time in Sydney and this proved to be a time of great joy to them. At their first meeting with the local church, Wilf told the people that he and Beth were their guests and while they were willing to help with preaching, the church was responsible for its own decision. During the year the church grew and the church leaders, both men and women, became active in handling their own affairs. At the conclusion of the year in Sydney, they attended the second SIL school in Melbourne and were surprised to receive an invitation to put their newfound interest in linguistics to work at Ooldea in South Australia.

Ooldea railway siding was on the Transcontinental Railway line that linked Australia's west and east coasts, and the mission was about 6.5km north of the siding. Pioneer welfare worker and lifelong student of Aboriginal culture and languages, Mrs. Daisy Bates, set up her camp at Ooldea siding in 1919 and served the people at the Ooldea soak. In 1933, Miss Annie Lock and a companion established a mission station at the soak under the auspices of the United Aborigines Mission.

Wilf, Beth and four-year-old son John arrived at Ooldea in open-window carriages drawn by a steam engine of the Trans-Australian Railway. After studying at the SIL school and Sydney University for a year, Wilf was prepared to discover the intricacies of what was to him, a new language. However, on meeting the superintendent, he was told all he had to do was rewrite material that had already been recorded. For the past year Wilf's world had been invaded by academic theories and intense lectures and discussions about phonetics and phonemics, which Dr. Ken Pike described as the science of alphabets; he had analysed recorded language data and studied morphology, syntax and anthropology; he had investigated sound systems and the structure of languages, and had read and listened to prominent linguists.

Ooldea Mission

Within a short time at Ooldea, Wilf became convinced that the English alphabet was not adequate for covering the significant sounds of the desert language and proceeded to find opportunities to listen to the speech of the Aboriginal people before attempting to write any data scientifically. Despite strong opposition from the mission superintendent, Wilf argued that the people were the custodians of their own language, and he needed to hear the language from the people.

He discovered that the mission woodpile was a favourite place for people to sit while they were waiting for rations of tea and sugar from the mission store, so would pull up a log of wood and, with pen and paper handy, join in conversations, writing down everything he heard. The superintendent didn't like his approach and argued that he was incorrect in his spelling, grammar and even how the words sounded, so Wilf usually developed two lists, the words written in the way his superintendent said they should be written, and another list with the words written in the way he believed they were being spoken.

Whether it was on the wood heap, surrounded by piles of logs of mulga wood, or in the mission camp sitting on dirty blankets and surrounded by dogs, Wilf's world began to unfold in a way he never imagined. He wrote down words from an ancient oral language that had never been written, least of all described scientifically, listening to the conversations, and beginning to grasp the grammar and the subtle differences between words and their meanings. He loved to go hunting for lizards with the children where he would be shown little clumps of bush in the valleys between the rolling sandhills and the blobs of gum on the trunks of the bushes; he would be told the names of the plants and the little birds that flitted from bush to bush.

As he listened and made notes, he became excited at discovering that the verb forms of the Ooldea language had an order and predictability that earlier linguistic studies had not seen. As he followed the children while they dug a lizard out of its hole, or opened the trapdoor of a spider, he sketched what he saw, and wrote the words next to the sketches, then, when he got home, would share his discoveries with the adults, making any corrections and noting subtle variations to the words. As he listened, it was as though a light had been turned on. By trial and error Wilf was discovering that these semi-nomadic desert dwellers, who had never seen the written word, had a sophisticated grammatical system to their language, as well as highly organised cultural laws.

But as exciting as the new world of language learning became to Wilf, he became depressed when he saw the way the mission was operating.

Only those Aboriginal people who attended church could receive the metal discs that made them eligible to obtain their government rations on that day. The boys and girls from the homes were taken to the church building, which doubled as a school and were seated on opposite sides of the building in their Sunday best clothes, boys on one side and girls on the other. Then the Aboriginal women were called in, mostly dressed in secondhand dresses in various stages of disrepair or cleanliness and were ushered down to the front to sit on the floor.

Wilf and Beth cringed as they saw the men, who were highly respected in their culture, lose all sense of respect in church as two cultures collided. The men were dressed in unkempt secondhand clothing that didn't suit their stature in society, and the children, all neatly dressed, giggled as they watched the men coming into the building. Most of the men wore a headband that was the symbol of manhood, sometimes covered by a beret or cap, but their head coverings would be removed with the warning that it was disrespectful to wear a hat in church. Men would try to sit down at the back of the building to avoid breaking the taboo about getting too close to their mother-in-law, but would be hastily pushed forward, being told not to worry about taboos, but to believe in the Lord Jesus and sit near the front.

Far away from civilisation, living in a wooden house surrounded by rolling sandhills that blew against one side of the house in the morning, then covered the opposite walls in the evening, Wilf and Beth were unaware they were at the centre of one of Australia's most controversial political decisions. While they thought internal mission politics were responsible for the news that Ooldea Mission was to be closed, little did they or the rest of Australia realise, that the Prime Minister, Robert Menzies, had revoked Ooldea's status as an Aboriginal Reserve to prepare for a joint exercise with the British government in testing atomic weapons in Australia's heartland.

The children's home was closed, the Aboriginal inhabitants of the mission were to be transferred to Yalata in the south of the state, and the missionaries relocated. For the next nine years, the desolate sandhills of Ooldea, on the Trans-Australian Railway Line were to become part of a prohibited area where the British government would conduct seven massive atomic tests, one of them, at least equal in power to the bomb that destroyed Hiroshima, along with hundreds of secret minor trials. Thousands of kilometres of traditional homeland of the Aboriginal people would be contaminated with radioactive materials for decades to come.

14
Writing the Stories

Untjima Forbes was only about nine-years-old when, for the first time, he saw a white person. He was born at a waterhole near the Jamieson community and moved into the Warburton Mission with his family shortly after it was established by Will Wade and his wife and family, on behalf of the United Aborigines Mission in 1932. Prior to that, as his family journeyed throughout the desert, walking from waterhole to waterhole, there were stories of a few light-skinned prospectors or "doggers" accompanied by camels, who had wandered on to their homelands, but for Untjima his life was little different from hundreds of generations of Ngaanyatjarra children before him.

By the time Wilf and Beth Douglas and their son John arrived at Warburton Ranges Mission, Untjima was about thirty years old and was one of the first people to meet Wilf and invite him to write down stories about his life and his knowledge of the local environment. The desert telegraph prepared him for this young missionary couple who had spent two weeks stranded on the road, but in that time had shown a keen interest in the local language and culture.

Day after day Wilf and Untjima sat on the ground under a tree to protect themselves from the blazing desert sun. The children played nearby and a nondescript dog stretched out to get as much of the shade as the two men would let them, opening its eye slightly from time to time to snap at an annoying fly that buzzed around its head. They told stories and laughed together as Wilf carefully wrote down words and phrases, regularly checking back that he had heard correctly what Untjima had been saying.

They never foresaw the day, thirty-eight years later, when the two men, a lonely Irishman sent off by his family to live on the other side of the world, and an Aboriginal man who traversed two vastly different cultures, would sit side by side on a stage at the front of a little corrugated iron church at the isolated Warburton Ranges Community, where a complete Ngaanyatjarra New Testament would be dedicated. Nor did they see the opportunities that Wilf would provide for two single missionaries, Amee Glass and Dorothy Hackett to undertake many years of tireless work towards the translation of that New Testament into a previously unwritten language.

As Untjima shared stories of his culture and they compared the Dreamtime stories with Bible stories, Wilf vividly recalled the letter advising him not to return to the Kimberley because his interest in language would return people to their heathen state. The memories were still fresh of the harsh criticism he had received in Ooldea because of his interest in language. So with all that behind him he had maintained a sense of caution, when shortly after arriving at Warburton he was told by the mission superintendent that he had been sent there to do language work. He tried a few times to organize some people to help him with language studies, and when those attempts failed he realized his doubts had proved to be valid. Finally, the superintendent admitted that the secretary of the mission had told him that while Wilf Douglas could learn the language for his own benefit, on no account was he to teach people to read and write in their own language.

Undeterred, Wilf took the view that he was the student and that the speakers of the language were the teachers and proceeded to sit with Untjima and others until he eventually became fluent in the use of the language. Early on he was asked to cut the men's hair, and as he snipped away at their hair he would start conversations that would enable him to hear words and phrases in their own language. He would write words on both the inside and outside of the box that his hair clippers were kept in, then at the end of the day would transfer all the information to filing cards and clean up the box, ready for more information the next day. He also noticed the large number of people who would come to the store to get their regular rations of flour, tea and sugar. Since he wasn't required to distribute the rations, he would sit on the ground with people and hear their stories. He had noticed that government workers, who weren't always trusted, would write in books, so Wilf took to writing on his hand as a mark of respect to what seemed a taboo issue for the people.

The Douglas home at Warburton Ranges

Wilf and Beth's home was a tiny slab stone house made up of a living section, a bedroom section and a breezeway in between. There was a wood stove, a small table and two or three chairs, and a few shelves in the living section. The floor was cement and the children would poke holes in the mud that held the rough-hewn stone slab walls together. Outside was a wash-house with a copper and a couple of cement troughs. An old tin bath, fairly open to the public, was situated at one end of the wash-house. They would avoid having bath time until after dark when the girls from the nearby girls' dormitory were locked up for the night and instead of the outside bath, used a small tub in the middle of the kitchen floor. When the cold winds blew through the kitchen, they would light a fire in a kerosene drum, place it on the cement floor and put up with the smoke for the sake of feeling a bit of warmth.

A team of children would round up and milk the goats each morning and a billy-can full of milk would be sent to them for John each day. The meat supply was mostly kangaroo, brought in by the men and sold to the superintendent who cut it up and sent it around the mission houses. Sometimes they would buy a kangaroo liver or a rabbit directly from the people. The mission had sheep and cattle, but one of the few times they recalled being offered mutton was a time when a missionary had found a carcass on the side of the road, but by the time it reached them it was crawling with maggots.

Church services were a little better than what they had experienced at Ooldea, but they quickly discovered there were some problems in relation to the way in which the message was being communicated. Christian meetings were usually in the open air on Sundays and other days when rations were being distributed. Everybody would turn up at church as rations were distributed after the services and fights would often break out during the service. The missionary in charge usually found a poster of a Bible story and would explain it privately to one of the young men who would stand in front of the crowd and re-tell the story in their language.

One of the missionaries quietly shared with Wilf some information that those who didn't know the language would not have appreciated. The Bible story was about the rich man and Lazarus. The interpreter had pointed to the picture of the fat rich man and explained that this was the mission superintendent who kept all the food, including the government rations in his house, and refused to allow the poor people outside to pick up even a crumb from his floor. Pointing to Lazarus sitting outside, he explained that this was obviously an Aboriginal person wearing old secondhand clothes like those distributed by the missionaries, and he had sores on his legs that were being licked by the dogs. One day, however, the situation would be reversed. The missionary would be out in the desert, not knowing where to find water. His tongue would be sticking to the roof of his mouth and he would cry to the Aboriginal, "give me water!" But the Aboriginal person would say, "No, you in your lifetime had all the good things and would not share them with us. Why should we tell you where to find water?"

Mr. and Mrs. Wade supported Wilf and Beth's desire to communicate adequately with the people, but Wilf observed that they didn't seem to respect the people's natural skills as hunters and gatherers, or their deep cultural attachments. To Wilf it seemed they regarded the Aborigines as poor people who had no natural food supply and were in need of rations, and who needed to have their naked bodies covered

with a great deal of clothing. Mr. Wade carried a few pieces of bread in his pocket and would stop a child and encourage him to say, "God is Love", then give the child a piece of bread from his pocket.

Wilf and Beth's house was situated next door to the girls' dormitory and since they weren't directly involved with the dormitories, tried not to openly express their concerns and observations about the concept of having Aboriginal children living in institutional care. With Wilf's experience of children's homes at Fairbridge and Sunday Island, he looked at the children from a different point of view than other missionaries and, in time, Wilf and Beth developed a reputation in mission circles as people who were opposed to children's homes. It came as a surprise to them some years later when Wilf was District Superintendent for the mission that he was asked to lead the process of closing the children's homes.

By that time, the Douglas family had moved to Kalgoorlie in the Western Australian Goldfields that was to become their home for nearly thirty years. Wilf regularly visited the various mission stations of the UAM in the desert region, Warburton Ranges, Mount Margaret and Cosmo Newberry, and as district superintendent had responsibility for each of these areas. Shortly after taking on this role, he visited Warburton Ranges and was told by two missionaries that he needed to close down the children's homes so they could concentrate on evangelism.

The missionaries were surprised when Wilf initially appeared opposed to the idea. His concern, however, was the effect of sending 120 children back to parents who lived in simple camps in the bush and had come to depend on government rations for sustenance. Furthermore, many of the children had been in the homes since they were babies and their parents had never had the opportunity to develop good parenting skills.

Wilf developed a proposal to close down the hostels in stages, starting with the younger children who had only been in the hostel for a short time and would not be shocked by the change back to camp life. The second group would be the children of parents who lived in houses supplied by the mission and had regular employment. The next group would be those who had regular employment, but who lived in the camps. The process would continue until the sixth and final group that would be those children whose parents were deceased.

The proposal involved considerable preparation and presentation by Wilf at a number of district conferences, but was finally approved, despite some ongoing opposition from missionaries who believed that children's homes were essential. The final step in the process was to meet with government officials in Perth to gain their approval, who, it turned out, had adopted a policy based on John Bowlby's book *Child Care and the Growth of Love* (Pelican 1955) in which it was stated (inter alia) "children thrive better in bad homes than in good institutions." The independent decision of the United Aborigines Mission to close down their Warburton Ranges hostel gave impetus to the new government policy to be implemented throughout the state. The government had begun to supply new buildings for the existing children's homes at Warburton so this was suspended, but plans to build a dining room/kitchen complex went ahead so children attending school could have at least one good meal a day until their parents were more economically able to support them. The opening of the new buildings didn't go without some difficulty. Before the dining room/kitchen was completed, two events occurred. A sudden cyclonic wind tore the building from its foundations and scattered aluminum sheets over a wide area and a measles epidemic hit the population of two or three hundred Aboriginal people which required the new dormitory to be turned into a three ward hospital.

Despite these issues, Wilf took leadership in bringing Warburton personnel together to help them understand how they fitted into the new plan for the future of the community. New teachers, building teams, new missionaries and other workers on the station were doing their own jobs without being aware how their contributions were part of the plan, so Wilf used his drawing skills to graphically explain what a consolidated community plan would look like, and brought the divergent workers and teams together to begin working together for the good of the whole community. A new sense of unity and direction was achieved as Wilf met with each of the personnel and through his drawings, explained where each of them fitted into the overall plan for the community.

15
Towards Independence

Wilf looked up from the bundles of filing cards scattered in front of him on the kitchen table. He could hear loud voices outside the stone slab house calling his name, but his mind was focused on the cards that contained hundreds of Ngaanyatjarra words, along with their meaning, and occasional sketches that illustrated the words. A separate word, or grammatical structure was written on each card. He looked across at Beth who was sitting on the other side of the table with their eight-year-old son John who was studiously working on his correspondence school lessons. Their world had begun to change when they had discovered the previous year that another child would be joining their family. Their second son, Robert was born while they were attending the 1954 SIL school at the outer Melbourne suburb of Belgrave Heights. The long journey across the Nullarbor Plain on the Trans-Australian Railway was still fresh on their minds as they looked at the baby sleeping peacefully in a basket in the corner of the room. The train journey was followed by an uncomfortable drive for Beth and a baby in the stifling cabin of the mission truck, with Wilf and John in the back, as they made their way over bumpy desert roads back to their home at Warburton Ranges.

Train trips to the Eastern States became a part of life

Visits to the SIL school had now become an annual event for three months at a time, as Wilf honed his skills as a linguist, no longer as a student but teaching subjects such as phonetics, phonemics and anthropology. The 1954 school had been significant for a number of reasons, not the least being Robert's birth. The Interdenominational Missionary Fellowship of Victoria had been running the SIL schools at Belgrave Heights each year from 1950 to 1954, and that year had marked the official launch of Wycliffe Bible Translators Australia. Harland and Mary Kerr, Bill and Lynette Oats, and Mary Short, all of whom had become close friends of Beth and Wilf, had left for the Philippines as the first Australians to join SIL/WBT's Bible Translation teams. In February of that year Queen Elizabeth II came to Melbourne, the first reigning British monarch to step on Australian soil, so Wilf and John, along with a heavily pregnant Beth found a place on the side of the road to watch the Queen drive past.

But for Wilf, even more important than the Queen's Australian tour was a visit to the SIL school of celebrated indigenous artist, Albert

Namatjira. Born at Hermannsburg Mission in Central Australia, Namatjira was the first indigenous artist to receive broad recognition in the art world, and during the Queen's tour was to receive the Queen's Coronation Medal for his highly celebrated work. His biographer, Joyce D. Batty in *Namatjira Wanderer Between Two Worlds* described Namatjira's visit to the SIL school in Melbourne and his meeting with Wilf. She said both men enjoyed the meeting immensely and Wilf showed a real love for the native language and culture. Batty said Wilf and Namatjira conversed fluently in a common Western Desert language and they compared items of vocabulary between Namatjira's Aranda and Pitjantjatjara.

Now they were back to the reality of life at Warburton Ranges and their memories of these recent events seemed far away.

The harsh winter wind blew in from the desert creating little eddies in the red dust, whipping up leaves and bits of trash into a willy willy that scooted across the mission compound. It swirled around the houses and blew through the breezeway of the little house. The slab walls were no barrier to the dust that seeped through hundreds of cracks and settled silently on the windowsills and bench tops and even on the baby's basket. Beth wiped her hands on her apron and sighed. She looked up at Wilf who was walking out to where the people were grasping at the cyclone wire fence and calling out for food. They were hungry, but so was she and she now had a baby and an eight-year-old to feed. She knew that Wilf's thirst for understanding the language of the people with whom he worked affected every part of his life, but that thirst competed with the hunger often experienced by a family who wondered at times where their next meal would come from.

As he approached the noisy group, other voices were calling to Wilf from inside his head. He knew the people were hungry, and keeping his own young family fed was always on his mind. He was also struggling with all the issues concerning the way the mission carried out its work. Why were these people no longer hunting for kangaroos or foraging for traditional fruits and berries? Traditional hunting skills had been replaced by regular hand-outs of rations from the mission store. The sight of a band of hungry people dressed in dirty recycled clothes challenged his thinking.

As he approached the fence he thought about the passages in the Bible that challenged him to give to those who were in need, but in that split second another voice said to him: "Give them back their independence." As he approached the group, one of the men lifted his shirt and invited Wilf to feel his stomach. The signs of malnutrition were showing and the man's bare stomach was a map to Wilf of the journey these people had taken from being independent hunters and gatherers to sedentary mission-dwellers, dependant upon rations of white man's food. Quickly, Wilf responded to the man by lifting his own shirt and inviting the man to feel his stomach. The group erupted in laughter and quickly headed off towards the superintendent's house to see if they would receive a better reception elsewhere. That was a turning point in Wilf's approach to mission policy.

The establishment of the UAM Language Department in 1958 marked a major step in the process of giving Aboriginal people back their independence. For twenty-five years, Wilf led this department driven by a passion held by both Wilf and Beth of providing people the opportunity to read the Bible in their own language. Following Robert's birth in 1954, the family had returned to Warburton Ranges where Wilf worked at gathering language material, and absorbed the culture and philosophy of the local people until moving to Mt. Margaret Mission where he founded the Western Desert Bible School and Translation Centre. Seven students attended the first course studying Old Testament, New Testament, Bible teachings, vernacular reading and writing and preaching. English, musical conducting, use of music and art in Christian service, and in addition, several portions of Scripture and a simple catechism were translated with the aid of the students.

Flying Doctor Plane at Warburton Ranges

At about this time, the new UAM Federal Secretary, Mr. Stuart Fowler started listening to Wilf's propaganda for Bible translating and indigenous church methods. Keith Morgan had supported him at Mt. Margaret, and had been transferred to Derby to superintend a children's hospital with his wife. Dr. Gibson, principal of the Perth Bible Institute also supported the idea of Bible translating for Aborigines and the indigenous principle. The three began writing articles on the subjects, encouraged by the world secretary of the Christian and Missionary Alliance, Reverend Louis King, a man who had taken great steps to encourage the indigenous church in Laos.

The family moved to Kalgoorlie in 1957 to set up a base for the language department, but shortly after moving, Wilf and Beth received a letter from one of the leaders of the Wycliffe Bible Translators, Dr. Richard Pittman (then stationed in Vietnam) suggesting they join SIL/WBT to open up Wycliffe's work among the Australian Aborigines. It was a tough decision. Wilf thought back on the amazing growth he had experienced as a result of his involvement with SIL/WBT, attending the SIL school in Melbourne each year since 1950. Through these experiences he had been introduced to the writings of Dr. Eugene Nida, a pioneer of translation theory and linguistics, the studies of Australian anthropologist Professor A. P. Elkin, and linguist Dr. Arthur Capell. His theology had been impacted by C.S. Lewis and he had met people like Graeme and Ella Smith; missionaries with the London Missionary Society in Madagascar, Harland and Marie Kerr and Bill and Lynette Oats, who had now gone to work in the Philippines. Even meeting Albert Namatjira had happened because of being in Melbourne at the SIL school.

He recalled Ken Pike's lectures on "Tagmemics", phonemics and morphology, his trimordal theories in linguistics and human behaviour and the opportunities he had with linguists and language informants from various parts of the world to record, analyse and describe languages. These were people who had changed his attitudes, moulded his thinking and opened up his mind and heart to the world of linguistics and Bible translation. These were people he could imagine working with for the rest of his life. It was a result of his learning through SIL/WBT that he had obtained the motivation and skills required to gain a foothold in the Western Desert and master the desert language. But since his time at Warburton Ranges his interest in mission policy had grown and as district superintendent of the desert area and with a voice at federal level, Wilf saw an opportunity to influence UAM policy, and it seemed that this was the wrong time to leave the UAM to join SIL/WBT.

For weeks, Wilf and Beth prayed about the possibilities and somehow the subject filtered its way into all their conversations. Then a letter came from UAM's Melbourne office indicating that Dr. Pittman had also written to mission headquarters asking for Wilf and Beth's release from UAM. The letter indicated they had told Dr. Pittman the mission was willing to second them to Wycliffe providing they remained in full standing with the UAM.

They made the decision. They would hold onto what they had gained in the UAM field realising to drop their work in the Western Desert would probably spell the end of the opportunity for Bible translation in UAM fields in the future. One of their Wycliffe colleagues, Bill Oates, ultimately initiated Wycliffe's work in Australia before his tragic death in 1968. The formation of the Australian Aborigines and Islander branch of SIL/WBT, centred in Darwin, would lead to translation and literacy programmes in up to thirty Australian languages.

In 1957, apart from the work of Ron Trudinger at Ernabella in the Musgrave Ranges of South Australia, there was little being done to give any group of Aborigines the Word of God in the language they understood best. It was with some surprise when Wilf and Beth received a letter from the Western Australian council of the UAM asking them to initiate a language department within the UAM. Apparently unknown to the WA council, the federal council in Melbourne was also writing to them recommending that they initiate a language programme. This letter arrived shortly after the one from Perth.

It seemed to Wilf and Beth that the request from Wycliffe's had convinced UAM council members that their vision had merit. The WA council had suggested that they form the language department to translate the Scriptures in the languages of the Western Desert and the Kimberley, a suggestion that coincided with their burden for the people of these areas. The UAM Language Department was officially formed in 1958 in the same year that the UAM's first Bible Institute was opened at Gnowangerup, Western Australia, with Don Milnes as principal.

***

Limerick was an Aboriginal elder living at Fitzroy Crossing, situated on the Fitzroy River, 200km east of Derby where Wilf had first begun delving into the Bardi language. Limerick spoke Walmatjari and was blind. When a young missionary with the UAM, Melvina Rowley moved to Fitzroy Crossing to take responsibility for a children's home, Limerick spent time with her helping to prepare simple gospel messages in Walmatjari and composed hymns in his own language using traditional music.

As the only members of the UAM Language Department, Wilf and Beth's first responsibility was to identify people who would be suitable as language workers within the department. Melvina had been a missionary on Sunday Island and Wilf's recollection of one of the UAM annual meetings in Melbourne was of her openly opposing his conviction that the Bardi people of Sunday Island needed the Bible in their own language. She later apologized to Wilf for her opposition saying following that meeting she had been challenged by God concerning her attitude.

On her return to the Kimberley, the UAM council sent her to Fitzroy Crossing on the mainland crushing Wilf's hopes of identifying his first Language Department member. Despite both his and her disappointment, Melvina began to record and analyse Walmatjari, the language of a desert tribe that had moved into the Fitzroy area. In 1958, Wilf travelled to Fitzroy Crossing and met Melvina who had, by this time, married Nelson Rowley and they had opportunity to study some aspects of Walmatjari grammar for which she and Nelson sought help. Wilf also met Limerick and discovered that he knew both Walmatjari and the dialect spoken at Warburton Ranges. The pair connected straight away as a blind Walmatjari speaker and a white man with Irish roots sat in the dirt near the Fitzroy River talking to one another fluently in the language of the desert people hundreds of kilometres to the south. In one afternoon they translated the Bible stories of the prodigal son and blind Bartimaeus into Walmatjari directly from the Ngaanyatjarra version that Wilf had translated previously.

Mt. House, Kimberley

The following year, Wilf was invited to the thirty-fourth ANZAAS Congress at the University of Western Australia on "The Vernacular Approach to the Australian Aborigines." The Australian & New Zealand Association for the Advancement of Science advocated the use of Aboriginal languages in education and communication generally, where the languages were used daily. Then, the WA State Conference of the UAM accepted Wilf's proposal for *The Acceptance, Appointment and Oversight of Full-time Bible Translators in the UAM*, and at the same conference Wilf was appointed chairman of a special committee formed to prepare a set of principles to guide missionaries into fostering the development of indigenous churches.

These opportunities set the newly formed Language Department on a sound footing both at a scientific and theological level, however, it was not until 1963 that two new missionaries to the UAM applied to join Wilf and Beth in this work. Amee Glass from Western Australia and Dorothy Hackett from South Australia underwent candidates' training course at the Douglases home in Kalgoorlie, launching what was to become, for them, a lifetime service in Bible translation in the central desert. Peter Taylor and Joy Faulkner who married each other after joining the Language Department followed them. Gwyneth Harrison was next to join the department followed by Herbert Howell and finally Lorraine Croot. Herbert and Lorraine also married each other after joining the Language Department. Apart from Gwyneth, all the team stayed with the Language Department for many years until theological differences with mission authorities led to significant changes.

The voice that challenged Wilf to give the Aboriginal people their independence had gone with him as he set about initiating approaches that would revolutionise mission thinking about the use of Aboriginal languages and the need for indigenous churches to be established. The significance of his achievements came home to Wilf one day as he was visiting a Warburton Ranges man who was taken to hospital in Kalgoorlie with a serious spear wound.

When Wilf first started visiting him, the man could only talk about how he could affect revenge against those who were responsible for his spearing. Day after day, Wilf visited him and shared God's word to him in his own language. As time went on a change began to occur, then during one of the regular visits he asked Wilf if he would help him write a letter to his father. Surprised at the request, Wilf agreed but was keen to find out what the man intended to say to his father. As they discussed the letter the enormity of the request began to take hold. Using his own language the man dictated to Wilf word-for-word what he should write to his father.

The letter stated: "When Jesus died on the cross they speared him but he said, 'Father forgive them for they know not what they do.' I want to forgive the one who speared me and not take revenge."

Croesus Mine, Kalgoorlie

16
Cycling the Goldfields

The gravel track wound around the outskirts of Kalgoorlie, skirting open mineshafts that had been dug and abandoned decades earlier by prospectors desperate to make their fortune from these rich gold-bearing soils. As he negotiated the winding track, Wilf was more anxious to avoid riding his bike down one of the unmarked shafts than to entertain any thoughts of being thrown deep into the bowels of the earth. Years later he was to appear as an expert witness regarding Aboriginal culture after a number of bodies were found dumped down mineshafts and as a result of his evidence, nine men were released from prison after being convicted, to receive a ritual spearing in accordance with their culture.

The old bicycle bumped up and down on the rocks as Wilf pedaled his way past another mineshaft, then headed through the bush to a humpy made of rusty pieces of corrugated iron, tree branches, and other pieces of discarded building material where he dismounted. He was at an Aboriginal reservation that was locally known as "the reserve", a bush location strategically located far enough away from the bustling Goldfields town to prevent embarrassment to the authorities, but close enough for the many Aboriginal families who preferred a semi-traditional lifestyle while benefitting from nearby urban facilities. Up until the 1960s, Aboriginal reserves were commonly established on the outskirts of towns with the primary goal of keeping Aboriginal people separated from the white population.

Wilf carried a small black bag full of Christian literature on his handlebars as he rode to the reserve each Sunday afternoon, and then on to the hospital where he could inevitably find a Christian tract in the language of whatever patient he met from nations all over the world. Language was the first point of contact for Wilf as he connected with Aboriginal people from many different language groups around Australia, as well as people of a wide range of nationalities. This habit, first by bicycle, and later by car, lasted for nearly thirty years, and also included regular visits to the prison where he would share the Christian message with prisoners.

On one occasion he was locked in a cell with sixteen prisoners, and it took some time before any of them could attract the attention of an officer to unlock the gate and let him out. In another instance he was locked in a padded cell with an old desert man who had tried to commit suicide. Wilf spoke to authorities on the man's behalf to be granted bail and return to his community where he could receive a ritual spearing, a result that seemed more appropriate than imprisonment. Beth would also visit the prison and hold Bible studies with the Aboriginal women prisoners.

The little black bag brought its own brush with the law on one of Wilf's regular trips to the reserve, at a time when evidence had been provided to the police that white men were trading alcohol for sexual favours. A quick look inside the bag by an inquiring police officer revealed the presence of booklets in multiple languages, but no bottles of sly grog.

A few oranges were stuffed into the bag for the family he hoped to see on this visit to the reserve—the relatives of a man who had died. The family was gathered outside the humpy in the shade of a tree, wailing according to Aboriginal custom for their departed relative. Wilf quietly sat down on the ground with them, bowed his head and joined in the customary wailing. As they expressed their grief, a procession of men and women appeared from the bush and stopped in front of the camp. Each of the members of the group was painted up for a traditional ceremony, markings on their faces, arms, legs and chest. The leading man stepped forward and demanded of an elder who was sitting with them, "Get that white fellow out quickly!" Immediately they were told, "It's all right, he's a *wati yirna* (an initiated elder). The leaders of the group accepted the old man's explanation and disappeared into the bush where they continued with the ceremony.

Following another death, Wilf was invited into a corrugated iron shed, the home of the grieving family. There was nothing in the shed except some rusty beds pushed against the wall and a fire of hot coals burning in the middle of the cement floor. The warmth created by the fire was a welcome break from the shivering cold outside. The door was shut, and Wilf was invited to pray with the group of people who sat on the floor around the fire. Apart from the crackle of the fire and the soft voices of those who were praying, the tiny room was silent. The door burst open and two police officers appeared. "What are you doing here?" they demanded of Wilf, the only non-Aboriginal person in the room. In a soft voice he responded, "Praying." Quickly, the police officers backed out, pulling the door shut behind them. A few days later one of the officers saw Wilf in town and apologised for the interruption.

The brush and corrugated iron humpies of the Kalgoorlie reserve, and the cold dark walls of the prison cells were one side of the life of a man who was respected by so many, but the demands on his time were many and varied. Members of the Language Department were at work on the translation of the Bible and he always saw it as a priority to provide leadership to these people and to be available to check their work. A check of the Christmas story in Ngaanyatjarra by

Amee Glass and Dorothy Hackett at Warburton Ranges was followed by a trip to Fitzroy Crossing to check Peter Taylor's work in the Kitja language and Gwenyth Harrison's Tjaru material. This was followed by a series of lectures at the University of Western Australia in Perth, then more lectures on the application of translating principles to Australian Aboriginal languages at the United Bible Society's Translator's Institute in Darwin. As a member of the Australian Institute of Aboriginal Studies, Wilf was in Canberra from time to time to present papers such as the "Aboriginal Categorisation of Natural Features". Then it was back home to run a candidates' course for new missionaries to the UAM. It was a special delight when Jonathon Bates and Bernard Newberry, two young Aboriginal men participated in the course in order to become missionaries with their own people.

For a number of years, Wilf wrote and presented short-term training courses in the Pitjantjatjara language at Adelaide University. The university's language laboratory provided each student with their own private booth with tape deck and earphones. Wilf always enjoyed new opportunities and delighted in the modern, high tech equipment that enabled him to teach an ancient language. He was an avid communicator who enjoyed discovering new ways of getting his message across. A duplicating machine was a standard piece of equipment in his office for mass-producing letters, brochures and other documents. A stencil was produced with a typewriter or stylus; this was placed on the drum, ink was applied and a handle was turned to allow the paper to be fed through the machine imprinting the paper with the ink that was pressed through the stencil. When electric typewriters replaced manual typewriters, it was an opportunity for experimentation. By replacing the type element, or "golf ball" as it was commonly known, the font could be changed. Wilf was adept with punch cards that were an invention said to have fuelled today's information revolution. He would write words or phrases on individual cards then would punch out the relevant holes along the edge of the card using an index that allowed him to identify parts of speech and other pieces of information he required. If he was looking for a verb, or an adjective, or a word with a particular ending, he would push a long metal skewer through the relevant hole in the bundle of cards, shake the bundle and all the cards would fall out that contained the information he needed.

Wilf's expertise and knowledge of both Aboriginal languages and culture were highly sought after over the years by linguists and anthropologists, but he maintained a healthy cynicism of anyone who placed their academic research above the needs of the individual. One day an anthropologist who was trying to identify sacred sites in the north eastern Goldfields and central desert area as part of a land rights project visited Wilf to obtain information for his research. The anthropologist laid out a large map on the table and asked Wilf to point out the sacred sites within a region of up to a thousand square kilometres. Wilf looked at the map and said to the so-called expert in sacred sites, "every square inch of ground in this area is sacred to the people who live there."

In 1964, Wilf's expertise attracted the attention of Professor Ronald Berndt of the University of Western Australia, a leading anthropologist and author of many scholarly works on anthropology and Aboriginal studies. Wilf's first experience with Aboriginal languages as a young man was with Nyungar, so it was a privilege for him to be given an opportunity to undertake a formal study of the Nyungar language. Professor Berndt invited Wilf to conduct a research project into the Aboriginal language of the southwest of Western Australia and at the same time undertake a lecturing appointment at the university's department of anthropology. For six months Wilf, who had never attended high school, would lecture for two weeks then spend a week doing field trips to collect language material. Using a spring-driven reel-to-reel tape recorder, he visited Aboriginal reserves and communities around the southwest of Western Australia, sitting with people for hours on end, listening to their stories.

He Speaks Our Language

University of WA, Perth

Ernie Dingo was just a lad when Wilf visited his home in Mullewa, a small town in the Murchison region of Western Australia. In time, he was to become a well known indigenous Australian actor and television presenter whose achievements included an AFI Award for Best Actor in a Television Drama, and a co-starring role with Cate Blanchett in the Australian television drama series *Heartland*. In 1997 he was named by the National Trust of Australia as one of Australia's 100 Living Treasures. Wilf had heard about Dingo's mother Bessie as one of the last speakers of the Watjarri language of the Murchison region, so took the opportunity during his research to visit Bessie at her home in Mullewa. Wilf sat in the kitchen of the Dingo home as Bessie and her children chatted about their life, sang songs together and shared their knowledge of Watjarri. Wilf faithfully recorded all that was said, both on tape recorder and in written form, preserving for posterity the details of a language that could have been lost forever.

Of the hundreds of indigenous languages that were spoken by Aboriginal people across Australia at the time of white settlement in 1787, many have been lost and are critically endangered. Wilf's research involved meeting with individuals who were among the last speakers of their language and represented a valuable rescue operation. His research into southwest languages took him to many of the places where Nyungar was traditionally spoken, but also led him into visiting towns north of Perth such as Geraldton, Mullewa, Mt. Magnet and Northampton to collect material on Nyungar, Watjarri, Patimaya and Nanta. The project resulted in Wilf writing important scientific descriptions of both Nyungar and Watjarri, two endangered West Australian languages.

Non-Aboriginal people are rarely granted access to cultural meetings, but during one of these visits Wilf was invited to a law meeting in Meekatharra where one hundred men gathered for a type of tribal court case. One of the issues raised was the practice of a Christian mission taking children from Wiluna and educating them at their mission station, allegedly encouraging them to break the Aboriginal Law by telling young people they could marry anyone they liked, regardless of the restrictions of the skin-grouping system.

In a report Wilf later wrote about this event, he described how the group of men kissed the sacred sticks then suggested "the white people have the Bible as their law and follow Jesus Christ, who was a white man. On the other hand, the Aborigines have their own sacred law and follow the *Wati Kutjarra* (The Two Men—heroes of the Dreaming).

Wilf was called up to reply to this interpretation: "As it happened, I had a copy of the prodigal son in the Western Desert language inside my shirt. I stood up, pulled out the portion of scripture and began to read it in the language. The passage began, 'Jesus said, a certain man had two sons...' I turned to the Strelley men and said, 'Some men here suggested that Jesus is a white man and that the Bible is a white-fellow book. Well, I'm reading from the Bible and it is in Wangka, (language) and the story Jesus told was about the subject which concerns you all ... a man who had one son who stuck to the law of his father and the other who went into a far country and mucked up. Jesus was not a white man, he was born in the middle, between the black and the white, so he could be a boss for everybody.' As I spoke, the Warburton men on my right raised their fists, in the manner the Strelley men had used previously, and shouted, 'That's right.'"

***

The scene of this traditional law meeting in the harsh conditions of the West Australian bush was worlds away from the ancient ruins of a Toltec temple not far from Mexico City. Only months after standing with law men who had upheld traditional values that had served their people for thousands of years, Wilf gazed past mighty carved pillars to see a pyramid, probably built about the same time as the Egyptian pyramids and beyond this a cathedral built by the Spaniards in the thirteenth century.

It was 1966, and the depth of Wilf's cultural and linguistic knowledge was challenged afresh when the opportunity came for him to attend a six-month language consultation at the Summer Institute of Linguistics Wycliffe Bible Translators (SIL/WBT) linguistic centre in Ixmiquilpan, 60km from Mexico City. SIL/WBT had paid for a return fare from Sydney to Mexico City and back, but at the time he had little chance of getting to Sydney to catch the plane. He had less than three weeks to organise visas, passports and vaccinations. Two days after getting the letter from Dr. John Beekman, head of Wycliffe's translation centre in Mexico, a letter came from the Australian Institute of Aboriginal Studies in Canberra inviting Wilf to attend their first biennial meeting. Enclosed were first class return air tickets to Canberra.

Wilf attended the local Otomi church in Ixmiquilpan each Sunday where he heard many stories from the local Christians. Religious fanatics had driven most of them out of their villages and men wielding machetes or rifles had attacked many. At one time, he was told, the local priest had called for a raiding party that would completely wipe out the believers.

In the dark of night, the signal was given to rush up the hill from all sides and kill everyone in the little church on the hill. Half way up the hill the raiding party was confronted by a band of soldiers in shining clothes and unable to move forward and overcome with fear; they retreated to the village. Next day in the market place the locals stared at the believers as they came to do their shopping, until someone asked, "Why did you hire the soldiers from the fort to surround your village last night?" The believers pointed out that there had been no soldiers in the fort since the Spaniards left Mexico, centuries earlier. They told their inquirers: "We were surrounded by an army of angels."

San Nicolas Church in Ixmiquilpan, Mexico

Wilf visited an isolated Christian home on the limestone plain where Modesto and his wife lived in a tiny house made out of limestone. Modesto's wife used a loom that was hung from a nail in the doorpost, to weave the fibre of the century plant into a cloth, called burlap, which was sold in the market for a few centavos. They had a few scrawny chickens in a little pen outside their house and when Modesto and his wife knew that Wilf would be returning to Australia soon, he caught one of the chickens, gave it to his wife and asked her to cook it for "our brother Douglas".

There was the time he and some others went to a nearby hill, and just below the surface were able to find pieces of pottery from the Olmec period, Mexico's first major civilization in about 1500 BC. On one occasion they found a tiny pot with a lid on it and inside were the remains of a newborn baby many hundreds of years old.

Everything about the trip filled Wilf with wonder and enquiry, but it was the language work that captured his mind. He was overwhelmed with the amazing experience of working with John Beekman, a veteran linguist, and listening to his explanations of the figures of speech that occur in the Bible and ways to translate these into other languages. He was given opportunity to check translations in many of the Mexican and Latin American languages and delighted in meeting indigenous men and women such as Nicholas, a Chol Indian; Venancio and his cousin Tito from the local Otomi group, speakers of Zapotego de Miahuatlan and Chichimeca-Pame, Chatino and Tephua, and other Mexican languages who had assisted these translators on the field and had now come to help with checking the accuracy of the language. While Wilf had been invited to contribute his valuable expertise to other translators, the trip was a reward for years of commitment to language study and added to the richness of a life lived in service for others.

Warutjarra, Blackstone Ranges

17
Desert Moon

A full moon was hanging like a huge glowing ball over the central Australian desert as a ragtag group crawled into their swags and settled down for the night. Their make-do beds were laid out on the ground, a semi-circle of bushes providing a barrier to the desert wind and offering a level of privacy from others in the group. Amongst them, an eighty-year-old Irishman lay in his swag, looking up at the moon and reflecting on the day that was now coming to an end. They had driven from Warburton Ranges across the Western Australian/Northern Territory border to Pangkupirri where they left their vehicle to walk through a deep valley of red rock cliffs set off by tall, white gum trees. They had found it hard to leave this magical spot after clambering up rocky walls to look into a deep, dark pool surrounded by green bushes and high rocks glowing red in the afternoon sun. Now they were camped at Yulpikarri in what was effectively the centre of Australia, 1600km northwest of Perth, 1300km southwest of Darwin and 800km west of Alice Springs.

The central desert moon was no stranger to this small bald-headed man and the gathering of Aboriginal Christians at an isolated bush camp was not an unusual event, but there was a sense of finality that rested on him. Here at Yulpikarri, he was surrounded by people who had been his colleagues for many years in translating the Bible into the language of the original Australians, along with those people who were there because of their thirst to hear the words of God in their own language. But it was to be the last time he would join the people he loved in this way. Only nine months earlier he had been diagnosed with cancer and now, as he lay on his back reflecting on a full life, he remembered a thought that had come to him a short time before: the idea of dying from cancer was not the right attitude. Rather, he was living with cancer and while he was still alive his work wasn't done. This was a life that had been packed full and if there were still things to be done nothing would get in the way.

It was another four years before Wilf passed away on the birthday of his eldest son, John, 22 March 2004. Beth died nearly two years after Wilf on 17 December 2005. Only two weeks before Wilf's death, colleague, Dr. Toby Metcalfe, published the fourth edition of the *Illustrated Dictionary of the Language of the South West of Western Australia*. Forty-seven years earlier, *Oceania* at the University of Sydney published the first edition of Wilf's *An Introduction to the Western Desert Language*, a description of the Western Desert language through the Ngaanyatjarra dialect spoken at Warburton Ranges.

At the time of Wilf's death, Steve Larkin, Acting Principal of the Australian Institute of Aboriginal and Torres Strait Islander Studies wrote to his widow and acknowledged Wilf's membership in the institute since 1964 until his resignation because of illness in 2000. He wrote: "Your husband's major contribution to the researching and teaching of Aboriginal languages in Western Australia— including Ngaanyatjarra, Nyungar, Watjarri and Bardi—is well recognised. His groundbreaking grammar of Ngaanyatjarra, published by the University of Sydney in 1964, remains to this day one of the most comprehensive studies of the Western Desert language. The illustrated topical dictionary of the same language, published by AIAIS thirteen years later, also stands as a testament to your husband's ongoing commitment to language maintenance."

Later that year Bill Edwards, who was superintendent of Ernabella Mission in the far northwest of South Australia (1958-1972), superintendent of Mowanjum Mission in northwest Western Australia (1972-73), minister of the Pitjantjatjara parish of the Presbyterian and the Uniting Church (1973, 1976-80), and lecturer in Aboriginal Studies at the South Australian College of Advanced Education and the University of South Australia (1981-96) dedicated a paper to Wilf's memory. The paper "Nyaa Tjana Wangkanyi? Interpreting for Aboriginal People in the Health Sector" was presented at the Triennial Conference of the Australian Institute for Aboriginal and Torres Strait Islander Studies in Canberra. He commenced his paper by stating: "Few if any non-indigenous people have shown such commitment to the cause of supporting, preserving, teaching and using Aboriginal languages in Australia over such a long period as did Wilf Douglas. He tutored me at a Summer Institute of Linguistics Summer School in 1958, and we remained in contact until his death. His enthusiasm, skill and humour inspired me and many others to persevere in learning and communicating in indigenous languages."

Wilf and Beth resigned from the United Aborigines Mission on December 17, 1982, after forty years with the mission. Differences with the mission hierarchy in the end became too much, but the result was that their ultimate goal was achieved. For many years, the mission letterhead designed by Wilf carried the words: Towards an Indigenous Church. This goal had come to fruition when the Aboriginal church at Warburton Ranges established the Ngaanyatjarra Bible Project on November 23, 1982 and invited Wilf and Beth to be their consultants; Amee Glass and Dorothy Hackett to be their translators; Herbert and Lorraine Howell to be literacy workers. The former Language Department members had been asked to leave the mission some time earlier over theological differences, so it was a great joy for all of them to come together again under the leadership of the local church including Alwyn Bates, Terry and Donny Robinson, Arthur Robertson, Brian Jennings, Gregory Fox, Carol Holland, and Tjingapa Davies.

On December 7, 1991, Wilf performed the dedication ceremony of the Ngaanyatjarra New Testament, *Mama Kuurrku Wangka Marlangkatja* (God's Last Word). The work was the culmination of many years of tireless work by Wilf's first candidates to the UAM Language Department, Amee Glass and Dorothy Hackett. Sitting on the platform of the little church at Warburton Ranges with him was Untjima Forbes, who thirty-eight years earlier was one of the first to teach Wilf his language.

In 2001, the Australian Council of the Bible Society in Australia awarded the Elizabeth Macquarie Award to Wilf in recognition of his lifelong contribution to the translation of the Bible into Aboriginal languages and in particular, his encouragement, advice, and inspiration to all involved in the Nyungar Bible translation project.

The award was named in honour of Elizabeth Henrietta Macquarie, who made a great contribution towards the availability of Bibles to convicts, Aboriginal people, settlers and visiting sailors in early Sydney, and influenced her husband Governor Lachlan Macquarie to call the meeting in 1817, at which Australia's first Auxiliary Bible Society was established. It was a fitting tribute for a lifetime of service.

Many cultures that have had a written language for centuries take their alphabet and other aspects of their language for granted. In 1990, a Nyungar Language Conference at Wellington Mills Camp Site near Bunbury was a profoundly powerful event for a group of people in the southwest of Western Australia who potentially could have lost both their language and their culture if critical work had not been done to reduce the language to writing. Nyungar language speakers from many parts of the southwest and as far north as Moora came together to discuss the issue of a common alphabet for all Nyungar dialects.

Wilf attended this momentous meeting and told of an elder from Kellerberrin who attended and at one stage walked out because he objected to the influence of some university linguists who had addressed the meeting. Wilf followed him out to see if he could help and recalled the elder turning to him and saying: "You are a Nyungar, Mr. Douglas, and can understand. All I want is to be able to afford a car so I can come down here and keep a check on these people to see what they are doing with our language." The group accepted some important decisions unanimously and a form of alphabet was accepted for the whole Nyungar area.

Wellington Mills was the culmination of a long journey from that first meeting with an Aboriginal police tracker at Fairbridge and the first words taught by Bob Mead at the railway siding at Badjaling. It was a journey of learning and listening that enabled him to hear words and cultural stories from the salt water people of the far north of the country, to the desert people living in the heart of Australia. This lonely boy from Belfast, who was to grow up with a passion to understand the languages of the original inhabitants of his adopted homeland and an even greater love for the custodians of these languages, would play a significant role in protecting some of these languages from extinction. Life at Fairbridge with all the pain of being separated from parents and the harshness of institutional life prepared him for experiences at sea and in the desert in the cause of sharing his faith with Aboriginal people and helping them find themselves and a God who spoke their own language.

18
W. H. Douglas Bibliography

1950   N'ul-N'ul. A brief description of the Nyul-Nyul language of the Dampier Peninsula, based on restricted information supplied by Dr. A. Capell and presented as an essay at the Department of Anthropology, University of Sydney.

1950   The Mixed Blood Community at La Perouse, NSW Australia, an essay presented to the Department of Anthropology, University of Sydney, as part of a Diploma of Anthropology.

1952   Hints on Art Work for Primers—duplicated booklet. Summer Institute of Linguistics, Australia.

1952   Printing Methods—duplicated booklet, Summer Institute of Linguistics, Australia.

1954   Wangka 1-5. A set of primers in the Ngaanyatjarra language. United Aborigines Mission.

1955   Phonology of the Australian Aboriginal Language spoken at Ooldea, S.A. 1951-52. Oceania, Vol. XXV No. 3. University of Sydney.

1956   Puntu Tjipututjara—the Blind Man. A translation of Mark 10:46–52 in the Mt. Margaret dialect of the Western Desert Language. Printed by J. D. Cochrane, NZ.

1957   'Ngatjil'. Fieldnotes collected from Eileen Flynn (Jacobs) 13 October 1957, Sentences and about 50 words of Ngatjumaya. IAAS 0196

          Nyakula Muntan—can you see? - Mark 8:22–27
          Wati Kurutjutu—the Blind Man - Mark 10:46–52
          Wati Pikatjarra Wilinyku—The man sick of the Palsy—Mark 2:1–12
          Katja Malaku Pitjantja—the son who came back—Luke 15:11–24
          (Four literacy leaflets in Ngaanyatjarra and English, printed by Scripture Gift Mission, London.)

1958   Purpa Jesusnga—the Lord Jesus—Ngaanyatjarra and English portions under the following headings; The Birth of Jesus; Jesus the Son of the Highest; Jesus, the Friend of Sinners; Jesus, the Good Shepherd; Jesus, the Giver of the Water of Life; Jesus tells about his Father's Love. Printed by SGM, London.

1958   An Introduction to the Western Desert Language, Oceania Linguistic Monographs No. 4. University of Sydney. A pedagogical approach to the Desert language. Revised 1964.

1959   The Vernacular Approach to the Australian Aborigines. A paper presented to the 34th ANZAAS Congress, Perth. Duplicated by the Dept. of Anthropology, UWA.

1959   Illustrated topical dictionary of the Western Desert language, UAM, Perth. Includes words from the Warburton area divided into three main sections, the people, their environment, and their culture (revised in 1977). IAAS 0164

1962 Bible Translating in Australia, in The Bible Translator, Vol. 13, No. 3, July 1962, United Bible Societies, Amsterdam.

1963 "Indigenous Christian Churches in Aboriginal Australia." A paper presented to the Inter-mission conference, Hermannsburg, NT.

1963 Katunya—God. An illustrated catechism, printed by Mission Publications of Australia. Later revised and published under the name Katungkatjana. MPA, Lawson NSW.

1964 An introduction to the Western Desert language, Revised. Oceania Linguistic Monographs No. 16, Sydney University, Sydney.

1967 Assimilation and the Use of Aboriginal Languages, in DNW Newsletter, Vol. 1 No. 3, December Issue, Department of Native Welfare, Perth.

1968 Pitjantjatjara course lecture notes, University of Adelaide, Adelaide. Outline of theory practice and comprehension methods, few notes on sounds, accents; 30 lectures for use with audiotapes prepared by H. J. Siliakus (BFC 721).

1968 The Aboriginal languages of South-West Australia: speech forms in current use and a technical description of Njungar, Australian Aboriginal Studies no. 14, Linguistic Series no. 4, AIAS, Canberra. Discussion of Nyungar, the name now popularly used for the languages of the South-West, of Neo-Nyungar, the contemporary blending of the original languages with English, and of Wetjala, Aboriginal English. An outline of the grammar and sound system of Nyungar is followed by texts and translations and an alphabetical word list of about 650 words.

1972 Dialect differentiation in the Western Desert—a comment, pp. 79-83 in Anthropological Forum, Vol. 3, no.1. A reply to W. Miller (1972b). The author claims that while there are distinguishable geographical dialect centres in the Western Desert, speakers may 'choose to contrast a different set of dialect idiosyncrasies or view the area under question from a different direction.' Because of movement between settlements, people's 'home' dialect becomes modified to the form of a 'universal accent.' IAAS 0084

1972 Linguistic routine report, November 1972. Notes salvage project in Watjari, re-examination of earlier data on consonants (AIATSIS).

1973 The language of southwestern Australia, pp. 48-50 in Journal of the Royal Society of Western Australia, Vol. 56, Parts 1 and 2. A brief description of the languages of the South-West drawn largely from the author's longer work on the same topic (Douglas 1968, republished as Douglas 1976b). IAAS 0184

1976 Aboriginal categorisation of natural features (as illustrated in the Western Desert), ts. Discusses ways of classifying the world in Western Desert languages. AIATSIS PMS2556

1976 The Aboriginal languages of the South-West of Australia, Australian Aboriginal Studies Research and Regional Studies no. 9, AIAS, Canberra. A revised version of Douglas (1968) including an English to Nyungar word list.

1977 Illustrated topical dictionary of the Western Desert language, revised edition, AIAS, Canberra. Revised version of Douglas (1959), includes words from the Warburton area divided into three main sections, the people, their environment and their culture.

1980 Comment on Margaret Bain's 'No Pitjantjatjara transformation', pp.327-330 in Anthropological Forum, Vol. 4, nos. 3-4. Supports Bain's (1980) analysis of Munn's work.

1980 Communication: Aboriginal languages—an overview, pp.39-53 in R. M. Berndt and C. H. Berndt, Aborigines of the West: their past and present, UWA Press, Perth. General introduction to Aboriginal languages, writing systems and applications to education.

1980 Review of 'Teach yourself Wangkatja [Vászolyi, E.G. (1979)], pp. 394-395 in Anthropological Forum, Vol. 4, nos. 3-4.

1980 The desert experience: language, pp.108-118 in R. M. Berndt and C. H. Berndt, Aborigines of the West: their past and present, UWA Press, Perth. Discusses dialect diversity in the Western Desert, introduction to the writing system, a short story from Ernabella.

1981 Watjarri, pp. 197-272 in R. M. W. Dixon and B. J. Blake, (eds), Handbook of Australian languages, Vol. 2, ANU, Canberra. A description of the Watjarri language originally spoken in the Murchison River area of Western Australia.

1982 Writing the South-West language, Mount Lawley College of Advanced Education, Perth. An introduction to the spelling system used for Nyungar and Wangkatha. IAAS 0171

1988 An introductory dictionary of the Western Desert language, Institute for Applied Language Studies, Perth. A dictionary that includes a topical, as well as an alphabetical listing.

1990 Illustrated topical dictionary of the Western Desert language, revised edition, Kalgoorlie College. Revised version of Douglas (1959 and 1977), includes words from the Warburton area divided into three main sections, the people, their environment and their culture.

1991 W. H. Atkins memorial Nyungar—English & English—Nyungar dictionary, [the author] Kalgoorlie. About 600 words recorded by Henry Atkins throughout his life as a missionary in the southwest of Western Australia.

1996 Illustrated Topic Dictionary of the South West Aboriginal Language. Edith Cowan University. Revised 2004.

No date available [Mirning word list].

No date available. Rules for the transliterating of proper names into the Western Desert language.
An aid to Bible translators, missionaries, and government officials ts. Provides rules for transforming English words into the Western Desert spelling system. AIATSIS PMS471

19
After-word

It was good to catch up with Myrtle Yarran again. A few years had passed since the pilgrimage I had taken to Badjaling with my two sons, and I wanted the opportunity to reflect with her on some of the stories I had been writing. She quietly listened as I read and every so often interjected with a comment. She was there when Wilf left Badjaling to join the army. She remembered the children standing on the platform crying as the train took their schoolteacher and friend away. A smile spread across her face as I read to her about how my father, Wilf Douglas, had met her father, Bob Mead, and how Bob taught Wilf his first word of Nyungar.

Wilf had always maintained that the Aboriginal people were custodians of their own language and culture and that it was a privilege for him to work with them in preserving language and using it effectively to communicate. When Bob Mead introduced Wilf to his first words, Bob's language had never been written and nobody understood the complexities of vocabulary and grammar. That young schoolteacher received Bob's gift, along with the gifts of many other Aboriginal people across Australia and over the years made it possible for their language to be protected and preserved in writing. And as he gave the gift back to them, he made it possible for their language to be the vehicle by which they would hear the words of Holy Scripture.

As this white-haired Nyungar elder and I spoke about the past, we knew that a connection had been established. The journey had started more than seventy years ago after a fox hunting expedition in the West Australian wheatbelt. As we reflected on the past, our discussion turned to the present. Myrtle and I had another unique link. In a juvenile detention centre in Perth, Bob Mead's great grandson now works as a unit manager. In the same centre, his colleague, the coordinating chaplain, is my son, Wilf Douglas's grandson. The journey continues.

20
About the Author

Rob Douglas is the son of veteran missionary/linguist Wilf Douglas and his wife Beth who served about 50 years in Western Australian Aboriginal mission work. "He Speaks Their Language" is the biography of Rob's father, based on memoirs that he wrote prior to his death in 2004.

Rob grew up in the West Australian goldfields and after leaving school became a journalist with the Kalgoorlie Miner newspaper. In two decades of regional journalism in Western Australia, including a period as a founding newspaper editor, Rob interviewed such people as Prime Minister, Malcolm Fraser, politicians Paul Keating and Don Chipp, heart surgeon Dr Christiaan Barnard, theologian Dr John Stott, author Erich Von Daniken, singer Marcia Hines and actor Warren Mitchell (Alf Garnett), and covered the royal visits of Prince Charles in Kalgoorlie, and Princess Ann in Derby.

In 2000 Rob was the national winner of a writing competition, Heritage Rave, organised by the National Heritage Commission, with a story about the history of the Carnarvon jetty.

Rob has an online book entitled Slices of Fruit which he self-published through Blurb books: au.blurb.com/books/1608009-slices-of-fruit

Rob has been a leader in the community services sector in WA and is currently, the team leader of the Maida Vale Baptist Church, Chairman of Hope Community Services an organisation providing drug and alcohol and youth services across Western Australia, and is a regular blogger: http://robdouglasblog.wordpress.com/

He is married to Robyn with two adult sons and four grandchildren.

www.ingramcontent.com/pod-product-compliance
Lightning Source LLC
LaVergne TN
LVHW051601070426
835507LV00021B/2694